100
GREAT ALBUMS
OF THE
SIXTIES

100
GREAT ALBUMS
OF THE
SIXTIES

Little, Brown and Company
Boston   New York   Toronto   London

A LITTLE, BROWN BOOK

First published in Great Britain in 1994 by Little, Brown and Company

A CIP catalogue record for this book is available from the British Library

ISBN 0-316-91056-2

10 9 8 7 6 5 4 3 2 1

Conceived, produced and designed by Brown Packaging Ltd
Colour reproduction by Classic Scan, Singapore
Jacket background based on *Blaze* by Bridget Riley
Printed and bound in Italy

Little, Brown and Company (UK) Ltd
Brettenham House
Lancaster Place
London WC2E 7EN

One breathless author would like to thank the following for their invaluable
contributions to this book: all at Brown Packaging, especially Ashley Brown, fellow
'60s veteran, for help in reliving the spirit of the age; Graham McColl for sensitive
editing and immense belief in the Rolling Stones; Sara Ballard for making sure the
entire enterprise got off the ground; Sandra Horth in Oz for design; Mal Stone for
photography; and Stasz Gnych for offering to sing the entire '60s repertoire of
Leonard Cohen. Many thanks also to Rachel Connolly at Little, Brown for some
sterling proofreading.
I am also indebted to Don Hughes, Andrew Lauder, Harry Shapiro and Eddie
Blower for the loan of record sleeves and Lynda Morrison for patience in the face
of adversity.
This book is dedicated to Al Kooper, who should do more, and my imminent fifth
grandchild.

John Tobler, 1994

CONTENTS

The '60s was the most innovative decade in 20th Century popular music. It was also the era that forced the long-playing record to evolve into a new art form – the album – at an incredible speed. The 100 albums featured here are those that best capture the way rock music developed and expanded to make those times so exciting.

The Beatles developed songwriting in a way that has yet to be matched. They were hugely influenced by Bob Dylan, who kicked down the saccharine-sweet facade of pre-'60s pop with his songs of politics, protest and drugs. The Rolling Stones sold black rhythm'n'blues back to white America, which had been ignoring it.

The different harmonies of The Who and The Beach Boys made their respective home territories of West London and the West Coast of America alluring to listeners from Stockholm to Sydney.

All of the albums included were released in the '60s, except the *Woodstock* soundtrack, which was released in 1970. The Woodstock festival took place in August 1969, and thus qualifies for inclusion. It is a fitting coda to a decade of experimentation.

Many artists who remain major international attractions in the '90s were just starting in the '60s, when they often released extraordinary albums. Ray Charles' *Modern Sounds In Country & Western Music* was the first country album by a black soul singer to top the US chart, while Johnny Cash's *Live At Folsom Prison* was the first platinum LP recorded with a literally captive audience. Tina Turner was still married to the violent Ike when they recorded *River Deep – Mountain High*, Lou Reed was in The Velvet Underground and Eric Clapton was in John Mayall's band.

The book also reflects the changing musical fashions of the decade, from the days when Elvis Presley and Cliff Richard were the respective superstars of the US and the UK, through the days of the twist and the period when instrumental acts like The Shadows were big stars, to the supergroups of the late '60s such as Cream and Crosby, Stills & Nash.

Those last two names bring to mind long, consciousness-expanding nights, but there were also albums that would push any party, then or now, in the right direction: Otis Redding's superb *Otis Blue*, James Brown shaking his stuff at Harlem's Apollo, Smokey Robinson and his Miracles…

Other black acts, such as The Supremes and The Four Tops, had their best work showcased on 'Greatest Hits' compilations without which no '60s record collection was complete; the same applies to white acts such as Donovan and The Hollies. Folk/rock, country/rock, jazz/rock and psychedelia all began in the '60s – the album format accommodated them well. Those pioneering sounds are as intriguing now as they were three decades ago. There's even *the* Christmas album – Phil Spector's girl groups adding a new dimension to the seasonal theme.

The albums are presented chronologically. This shows the rise of the album as the decade progressed. Almost half the selections are from 1968 and 1969; the first five years provide less than 20% of the 100.

The selections were my choices, so if your favourite '60s album is missing, I'm to blame…

JOHN TOBLER

ELVIS IS BACK!

ELVIS PRESLEY (1960)

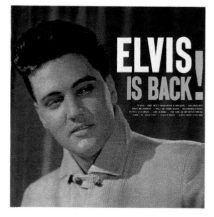

Produced by Chet Atkins
Total running time: 32.18
Released in the US & UK by RCA Records

SIDE ONE
Make Me Know It (Otis Blackwell)
Fever (John Davenport/Eddie Cooley)
The Girl of My Best Friend
(Beverly Ross/Sam Bobrick)
I Will Be Home Again (Benny
Benjamin/Raymond Leveen/Lou Singer)
Dirty, Dirty Feeling (Jerry Leiber/Mike Stoller)
Thrill Of Your Love (Stanley Kesler)

SIDE TWO
Soldier Boy (David Jones/Theodore Williams)
Such A Night (Lincoln Chase)
It Feels So Right (Fred Wise/Ben Weisman)
The Girl Next Door Went A-Walking
(Bill Rice/Thomas Wayne)
Like A Baby (Jesse Stone)
Reconsider Baby (Lowell Fulson)

A lot was expected of this first album by 'The King' after his discharge from the US Army. Over the previous two years, RCA had been forced to supply the demand from Elvis fans with a handful of 'new' (unheard) tracks recorded before he became Private US53310761. It was vital that his first post-Army work should be up to the high standard of his previous output, and this, his first LP of the decade, was his best of the '60s.

Elvis used material by writers whose songs had been successful for him in the past, like Otis Blackwell, writer of 'All Shook Up' and 'Don't Be Cruel' and Leiber & Stoller, who had provided 'Jailhouse Rock', 'Hound Dog' and 'Loving You'. He was backed by guitarists Scotty Moore (from his first band) and Hank Garland, Floyd Cramer (piano), Bob Moore (bass) and either D.J. Fontana or Buddy Harman on drums. Vocal backing came from The Jordanaires and sax star Homer 'Boots' Randolph was on some tracks.

Presley proved that Uncle Sam had not removed all his spirit along with his hair. Among the standout tracks are 'Such A Night' (a 1954 UK Number 1 by Johnny Ray), 'Fever' (a 1956 US hit for Little Willie John, but here in the style of Peggy Lee's 1958 hit version) and bluesman Lowell Fulson's plea to 'Reconsider Baby'. *Elvis Is Back!* surprisingly failed to top the US chart, being held off by the pop/folk of *Sold Out* by The Kingston Trio, but it was the first UK Number 1 album by Presley.

BAD BUSINESS

During the first eight years of the '60s, virtually all Presley's albums after this one (apart from 'Greatest Hits' collections and, ironically, two religious albums) were disposable.

Periodically, he released singles of good quality, such as 'It's Now Or Never' (1960), 'Are You Lonesome Tonight' and 'His Latest Flame' (1961), 'Return To Sender' (1962) and 'Devil in Disguise' (1963).

Presley's artistic decline during the '60s is often blamed on his manager, 'Colonel' Tom Parker. Parker decided that the best way to satisfy Elvis's fans would be via feature movies, which could be seen all over the world, obviating the necessity for live appearances.

On paper, there was an obvious logic to this approach. However, Parker's business acumen did not stretch to the realisation that the public would not tolerate indefinitely films with transparent plots and sub-standard songs, a category into which the majority of Elvis's 27 movies released between 'G.I. Blues' (late 1960) and 'Change Of Habit' (January 1970) sadly fell.

Presley himself eventually realised that his popularity was on the wane. He returned to live performance for an acclaimed TV Special in 1968 and 1969's live album, From Memphis To Vegas.

ANOTHER SMASH

THE VENTURES (1961)

SIDE ONE
Riders In The Sky (Jones)
Wheels (Petty)
Lonely Heart (Bogle/Wilson)
Bulldog (Tomsco)
Lullaby Of The Leaves (Petkere/Young)
Beyond The Reef (Pitman)

SIDE TWO
Rawhide (Grant/Wray)
Meet Mister Callaghan (Spear)
Trambone (Atkins)
Last Date (Cramer)
Ginchy (Weedon)
Josie (Bogle/Wilson)

Produced by Josie Wilson & Bob Reisdorff
Total running time: 28.15

Released in the US on Dolton Records and in the UK on London Records

In early '60s UK, The Shadows inspired many to take up the guitar. Their US equivalent was The Ventures, formed in Seattle in 1959 by Bob Bogle and Don Wilson. Recruiting Nokie Edwards, first on bass, later as lead guitarist when Bogle switched to bass, and drummer Howie Johnson, their debut 1960 single was on their own Blue Horizon label, overseen by Wilson's mother, Josie, as The Versatones.

They soon established a formula which maintained their popularity in the US throughout the '60s and beyond – instrumental cover versions of tunes which had often been hits for others.

The group evolved a 'Ventures sound', enabling them to adapt and perform virtually anything with little rehearsal and record whole albums very quickly: in 1961, four Ventures LPs reached the US chart. *Another Smash* was the third. It remains the best example of a sound that inspired thousands.

Like its predecessors, it included a US hit single, 'Lullaby Of The Leaves', a 1932 US chart-topper for George Olsen & His Orchestra, but half the album was more contemporary.

'Wheels', written by Norman Petty (Buddy Holly's producer), had been a 1961 hit for The String-A-Longs, 'Trambone' was a well-known Chet Atkins tune, 'Ginchy' was a UK hit for Bert Weedon, and country piano star Floyd Cramer's 'Last Date' had reached the US Top 3.

SUCCESSFUL VENTURES

In the '60s, The Ventures released 33 albums which reached the US chart, including an instructional album, 1965's Play Guitar With The Ventures. *Over half these albums reached the Top 40; 28 of the 33 were in the chart for at least 12 weeks, sustained success that few acts have equalled – an average of least three hit albums a year for an entire decade. In 1963 alone, they sold a million LPs.*

The sleeve notes to a 1973 compilation album by the group accurately described their appeal thus: 'Guitars played with little flash, hardly any improvisation but with a superb sense of melody and space.' They were also innovative – their 1962 US hit, 'The 2,000 pound Bee', used a fuzzbox effect which was virtually unknown at the time.

In 1963, Howie Johnson was seriously injured in a car accident and was forced to give up playing. He was replaced by Mel Taylor. At the same time, Bob Bogle and Nokie Edwards swapped instruments, but the sound remained the same, as did the formula. When the British Invasion filled the US charts with dozens of beat groups The Ventures began to travel – particularly to Japan. By 1973, they had released 13 albums exclusively for the Japanese market and had sold 30 million records!

HEY LET'S TWIST
ORIGINAL SOUNDTRACK

JOEY DEE & THE STARLITERS (1962)

SIDE ONE
Hey Let's Twist (Glover/Dee/Levy) (1)
Roly Poly (Glover/Dee/Levy) (2)
I Wanna Twist (Glover/Dee/Levy) (3)
Peppermint Twist Part 1 (Glover/Dee) (1)
Keelee's Twist (Glover/Dee/Levy) (4)
It's A Pity To Say Goodnight (Billy Reid) (5)

SIDE TWO
Mother Goose Twist
(Randazzo/Weinstein/Barbariss) (5)
Joey's Blues (Glover/Dee/Levy) (6)
Let Me Do My Twist (Glover/Dee/Levy) (7)
Blue Twister (Glover/Dee/Levy) (8)
Shout (Isley Brothers) (1)
Na Voce, Na Chitarra E 'O Poco 'E Luna
(Stillman/Rossi/Calise) (3)

THE ARTISTS
(1) Joey Dee & The Starliters, (2) Joey Dee,
(3) Kay Armen, (4) The Starliters, (5) Teddy
Randazzo, (6) Dave & The Starliters,
(7) Jo-Ann Campbell, (8) Bill Rammel

Produced by Henry Glover
Total running time: 39.40
Released in the US by Roulette Records and
in the UK by Columbia Records

long with Chubby Checker, Joey Dee (real name Joseph DiNicola) was a titan of the twist, although its originator was Hank Ballard, who in 1959 wrote and recorded 'The Twist', which reached the US Top 30.

A year later, a young Fats Domino fan named Ernest Evans covered the song. Slightly overweight, he used the name Chubby Checker, and the single was a smash hit, topping the US chart in September 1960, just as a five piece band from New Jersey, Joey Dee & The Starliters, began a residency at a New York club, the Peppermint Lounge.

There, local trendsetters demanded to twist. When vocalist Dee responded, the club became immensely popular, and the group signed to Roulette Records.

Dee and record producer Henry Glover wrote 'Peppermint Twist', a song which publicised both the club and the dance, and which topped the US chart at the start of 1962.

Dee swiftly charted with two more twist hits in the next six weeks, 'Hey Let's Twist' (US Top 20) and a cover version of a 1959 Isley Brothers hit, 'Shout' (US Top 10).

'From the temple of Twist where it all began – New York's famous Peppermint Lounge – comes the first motion picture about the sensation that has the whole nation in a rhythmic uproar' screamed this soundtrack album's sleeve note, referring to the first dance craze of the '60s, the twist.

The album captured the relatively innocent energy and excitement of the early '60s. Its unrelenting rhythm made it a US Top 20 hit.

TWISTING TO THE TOP

After 'The Twist' topped the US chart in 1960, Chubby Checker released 'Let's Twist Again' in mid-1961, which not only reached the US Top 10 but also brought 'The Twist' back into the chart and eventually to Number 1, making it the only single other than Bing Crosby's 'White Christmas' to re-enter the US chart and return to Number 1, where it was replaced by Dee's 'Peppermint Twist'.

The original line-up of The Starliters, with organist Carlton Latimer, drummer Willie Davis and backing vocalists Larry Vernieri & David Brigati, played on Dee's first five hits, including 'Roly Poly', and 'What Kind Of Love Is This' from another movie, 'Two Tickets To Paris'.

But by early 1963, the twist was dead. Dee had accumulated seven US hit singles in just over a year and the group's only three US hit LPs came in just over six months. It was a phenomenon which indeed lived fast and died young.

MODERN SOUNDS IN COUNTRY & WESTERN MUSIC

RAY CHARLES (1962)

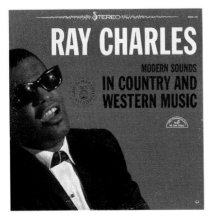

Produced by Sid Feller
Total running time: 39.12

SIDE ONE
Bye Bye Love (F. Bryant/B. Bryant)
You Don't Know Me (C. Walker/E. Arnold)
Half As Much (C. Williams)
I Love You So Much It Hurts (F. Tillman)
Just A Little Lovin' (Z. Clements/E. Arnold)
Born To Lose (F. Brown)

SIDE TWO
Worried Mind (J. Davis/T. Daffan)
It Makes No Difference Now
(J. Davis/F. Tillman)
You Win Again (H. Williams)
Careless Love (Ray Charles)
I Can't Stop Loving You (D. Gibson)
Hey Good Lookin' (H. Williams)

Released in the US by ABC-Paramount
Records and in the UK by HMV Records

Known as one of America's foremost soul/R&B artists, vocalist and pianist Ray Charles, who had been blind since the age of seven, broke new ground with this remarkable album.

It was the first country album by a black artist to top the US pop chart, where it remained for 14 weeks.

Charles (born Ray Charles Robinson in Georgia) had moved from Atlantic Records, where he first came to fame during the '50s, to ABC-Paramount, whose very generous offer of a large advance and ownership of the records was impossible to refuse.

Always ready to experiment – his 1961 US Top 5 LP, *Genius + Soul = Jazz*, found him backed by Count Basie's band – he asked producer Sid Feller to suggest enough country songs for an LP, on which he was backed by a big band, with arrangements by Gerald Wilson & Gil Fuller on some tracks and by a string section, arranged by Marty Paich, on others.

The album featured his soulful versions of Eddy Arnold's 'You Don't Know Me' (a million-selling Top 3 US pop chart hit for Charles) and 'Just A Little Lovin' ' and two songs written by Floyd Tillman, his 1948 US Country Top 5 hit, 'I Love You So Much It Hurts' and 'It Makes No Difference Now'. He also covered a pair of famous Hank Williams classics.

Best-known, perhaps, is the unforgettable two-million-selling version by Charles of Don Gibson's 'I Can't Stop Loving You' with a huge choir, which topped the US singles chart for five weeks. There was even a cover of the first big hit by The Everly Brothers, 'Bye Bye Love'. The album was instantly successful, remaining in the US chart for over 100 weeks. It was also Charles's only UK Top 10 album.

A BATTLER

After studying music at St. Augustine's School For The Deaf & Blind in Florida, Charles became extremely successful during the '60s, with 26 albums and 59 singles reaching the US chart during the decade.

He also became involved with illegal drugs, first being arrested in 1964, and in 1966 received a five year suspended sentence for possession of heroin and marijuana.

Sadly, these aberrations distracted attention from his undoubted talent in many areas of music – after he cured himself during a lengthy sabbatical, he admitted that he had been using drugs since 1945.

Ray Charles has strongly influenced two younger superstars. Stevie Wonder is similarly blind, but Charles's example of becoming world-famous despite his disability encouraged Wonder to do likewise. And Joe Cocker, one of the world's most soulful singers, cites Charles as his major vocal inspiration.

While Modern Sounds In Country & Western Music is a great album, it is just one of several styles at which Charles has excelled.

GREEN ONIONS

BOOKER T. & THE M.G.S (1962)

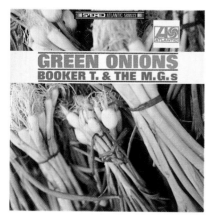

SIDE ONE

Green Onions (Booker T. Jones/Steve Cropper/Al Jackson/Lewis Steinberg)
Rinky-Dink (David Clowney/Paul Winley)
I Got A Woman (Ray Charles)
Mo' Onions (Booker T. Jones/Steve Cropper/Al Jackson/Lewis Steinberg)
Twist & Shout (Phil Medley/Bert Russell)
Behave Yourself (Booker T. Jones/Steve Cropper/Al Jackson/Lewis Steinberg)

SIDE TWO

Stranger On The Shore
(Acker Bilk/Robert Mellin)
Lonely Avenue (Doc Pomus)
One Who Really Loves You
(William Robinson)
You Can't Sit Down
(Dee Clark/Cornell Muldrow)
A Woman, A Lover, A Friend (Sid Wyche)
Comin' Home Baby (Ben Tucker)

Produced by Jim Stewart
Total running time: 34.58
Released in the US by Stax Records and in the UK by London Records

All the tracks here feature memorable interplay between Booker T. Jones's organ and Steve Cropper's guitar above the rock solid rhythms of drummer Al Jackson and Lewis Steinberg on bass. It remains one of *the* sounds of the '60s.

This quartet of session musicians had frequently worked at Stax Records studios in Memphis. One of them, guitarist Cropper, was also a member of The Mar-Keys, a studio group which had reached the US Top 3 in 1961 with the funky 'Last Night'.

Booker T. & The M.G.s (an abbreviation of 'Memphis Group') recorded their first instrumental tracks, 'Behave Yourself' and 'Green Onions', after completing a studio session with rockabilly star Billy Lee Riley.

Stax boss Jim Stewart thought 'Behave Yourself' had potential as a single, but when it came out on a Stax subsidiary, Volt Records, the B-side, 'Green Onions', attracted radio play and the single was

reissued, whereupon it sold a million copies and reached the US Top 3.

Three months later, this album, titled after the hit single, was released and peaked within the US Top 40. Although the single was not a UK hit at the time, it established a cult following for the quartet, and the album was belatedly released in the UK in mono by London Records in 1964, when it almost reached the Top 10. Within a year, London had lost the rights to release Stax product, and in late 1966 it was reissued by Atlantic Records, again in mono – the first UK stereo version appeared in late 1969.

Apart from the two tracks on the single, the album included covers of well-known instrumentals such as 'You Can't Sit Down', a 1961 US Top 30 hit by the Phil Upchurch Combo, 'Rinky-Dink', a 1962 US Top 10 hit for Dave 'Baby' Cortez and even 'Stranger On The Shore', the 1962 million-seller by English clarinet player Acker Bilk.

A YOUTHFUL TALENT

Booker T. Jones, a musical prodigy who directed his school band (another member of which was Earth, Wind & Fire leader Maurice White), received the accolade of inclusion in the 'Who's Who Of American High Schools'.

As a teenage student, Jones played organ on many Stax recording sessions, and after-hours jam sessions with Cropper after recording dates revealed considerable musical compatibility despite Jones being black and Cropper white – when 'Green Onions' was heard in Britain, it was widely presumed that Cropper must be black. Bass player Steinberg left the group in 1964. Drummer Jackson was shot dead in Memphis in 1975.

SUMMER HOLIDAY

CLIFF RICHARD & THE SHADOWS (1963)

Produced by Norrie Paramor
Total running time: 44.31
Released in the UK on Columbia Records

SIDE ONE
Seven Days To A Holiday (Myers/Cass) (1)
Summer Holiday (Welch/Bennett) (2)
Let Me Take You For A Ride (Myers/Cass) (1)
Les Girls (Welch/Marvin/Bennett) (3)
Round And Round (Welch/Marvin/Bennett) (3)
Foot Tapper (Marvin/Welch) (3)
Stranger In Town (Myers/Cass) (1)
Orlando's Mime (Stanley Black) (4)

SIDE TWO
Bachelor Boy (Richard/Welch) (2)
A Swingin' Affair (Myers/Cass) (5)
Really Waltzing (Myers/Cass) (1)
All At Once (Myers/Cass) (1)
Dancing Shoes (Welch/Marvin) (2)
Yugoslav Wedding (Myers/Cass) (4)
The Next Time (Kaye/Springer) (2)
Big News (Richard/Conlin/Cass) (2)

ARTISTS
(1) Cliff Richard with the Associated British Studio Orchestra conducted by Stanley Black, (2) Cliff Richard & The Shadows, (3) The Shadows, (4) Associated British Studio Orchestra, (5) Cliff Richard with Grazina Frame and The Associated British Studio Orchestra.

In the late '50s and early '60s, before The Beatles emerged as the biggest British act of the postwar era, Cliff Richard reigned unchallenged as the most popular home-grown rock star.

Basing himself on Elvis Presley's blueprint, by 1960 Richard had followed Presley's post-US Army direction: many of his hits were less uninhibited, as he was pushed (willingly) towards gentler material. His appeal had always involved his backing group, The Shadows (originally The Drifters – the new name was adopted to avoid confusion with the US R&B group), who were the equivalent of a polite teenage gang with Richard as their leader.

Launching Richard in films was a predictable step, and in 1959 Cliff's screen career had started with a role as a young tearaway in 'Serious Charge' starring Anthony Quayle, and it continued along similar lines later that year in 'Expresso Bongo', starring Laurence Harvey.

In 1960, The Shadows emulated Cliff's chart-topping success with their own 'Apache'. Thereafter it was an obvious move for the group to appear with him on the big screen.

The 1961 movie soundtrack *The Young Ones* was so successful that the same team worked on *Summer Holiday*, released in early 1963. The project produced four UK Number 1 hits, 'The Next Time', 'Bachelor Boy' and 'Summer Holiday' by Cliff with The Shadows, and 'Foot Tapper' by The Shadows alone.

The plot of the film was lightweight, with the group travelling across Europe to Greece in a red London bus, but it was a huge success at the box office.

ROLE MODELS

The Shadows had been Cliff Richard's backing group since late 1958, when their most famous line-up: Hank B. Marvin (lead guitar), Bruce Welch (rhythm guitar), Terence 'Jet' Harris (bass) and Tony Meehan (drums), assembled.

The group's most significant achievement was in being role models for future generations of British groups. Among major latterday names who have cited Hank Marvin (real name Brian Rankin) as an early influence are Neil Young and Mark Knopfler of Dire Straits, who, along with Jeff Lynne (of The Move, The Electric Light Orchestra, The Travelin' Wilburys, etc.), joined Marvin in 1993 to record a new version of 'Wonderful Land', which had been a 1962 UK Number 1 for The Shadows.

PLEASE PLEASE ME

THE BEATLES (1963)

Produced by George Martin
Total Running Time: 32.48
Released in the UK on EMI/Parlophone

SIDE ONE
**I Saw Her Standing There
(McCartney/Lennon)
Misery (McCartney/Lennon)
Anna (Go To Him) (Alexander)
Chains (Goffin/King)
Boys (Dixon/Farrell)
Ask Me Why (McCartney/Lennon)
Please Please Me (McCartney/Lennon)**

SIDE TWO
**Love Me Do (McCartney/Lennon)
P.S. I Love You (McCartney/Lennon)
Baby It's You
(David/Williams/Bacharach)
Do You Want To Know A Secret
(McCartney/Lennon)
A Taste Of Honey (Scott/Marlow)
There's A Place (McCartney/Lennon)
Twist And Shout (Medley/Russell)**

Please Please Me was a major milestone in rock history both culturally and statistically.

It was the first studio album by The Beatles, the band who redefined the long-playing record. It also remained at the top of the UK album chart for 30 consecutive weeks, an achievement that, over 30 years later, still remained unequalled by a rock album.

The inclusion of five cover versions (over one third of the album) may seem an indication that the group and George Martin were understandably insecure, despite the hit-single status of both 'Love Me Do' and 'Please Please Me' – it was their debut album, after all.

But the real reason for including so many covers was that the group needed to record ten tracks in a single day, 11 February 1963.

It was therefore expedient to record material they used in their stage act. The Beatles were a well-rehearsed live band at the time, as ten finished tracks in one 16-hour day indicates.

The album cost £400 to record, and unfortunately it sounds like it – the stereo mix (it was recorded using only two tracks) has the vocals on one side and the backing on the other.

The CD release magnified the album's technical shortcomings, but the group's spirit, drive, ambition and hunger remained clear.

Live versions of both 'Twist And Shout' and 'A Taste Of Honey' had been primitively recorded by fellow-Liverpool R&B musician Ted 'King Size' Taylor in Hamburg two months earlier. Taylor's mono tape (released years later) also included 'I Saw Her Standing There'.

ORIGINS OF COVER VERSIONS

'Anna (Go To Him)' was written and recorded by black American R&B singer Arthur Alexander (who also provided The Rolling Stones with 'You Better Move On'). 'Chains' was a US Top 20 hit for The Cookies in 1962/3. 'Boys' was the B-side to the million-selling 'Will You Love Me Tomorrow' by black girl group The Shirelles, which topped the US chart in 1961. 'Baby It's You' was also a hit for The Shirelles, reaching the US Top 10 in 1962. 'A Taste Of Honey' was the title tune to a play of that name, which was later made into a feature film.

The first US release of this album in 1963 was titled Introducing The Beatles *and omitted 'Please Please Me' (hence the need for a different title) and 'Ask Me Why'. These tracks were included when it was re-issued in 1965 as* The Early Beatles, *but 'I Saw Her Standing There' and 'There's A Place' were omitted. This album first appeared in the US in identical form to the UK original in 1978, as part of a limited edition 13 LP boxed set, and only became widely available in the US in 1987, when all the Beatles' albums appeared on CD.*

LIVE AT THE APOLLO, 1962

JAMES BROWN (1963)

Produced by James Brown
Total running time: 31.36
Released in the US on King Records and in the UK on London Records

SIDE ONE
I'll Go Crazy (Brown)
Try Me (Brown)
Think (Pauling)
I Don't Mind (Brown)
Lost Someone (Part One)
(Brown/Byrd/Stallworth)

SIDE TWO
Lost Someone (Part Two)
(Brown/Byrd/Stallworth)
Please, Please, Please (Brown/Terry)
You've Got The Power (Brown/Terry)
I Found Someone (Brown/Stallworth/Byrd)
Why Do You Do Me (Byrd/Keels)
I Want You So Bad (Brown)
I Love You Yes I Do (Nix/Glover/Seiler/Wood)
Why Does Everything Happen To Me
(Hawkins/Taub)
Bewildered (Powell/Whitcup)
Please Don't Go (Brown/Terry)
Night Train (Forrest/Washington/Simpkins)

James Brown remains one of the most revered black artists in modern popular music and *Live at the Apollo* is testimony to his greatness.

Financed by Brown himself (because King Records, the label to which he was signed, regarded a live LP from someone whose studio LPs had failed to reach the chart as an unacceptable risk), this was his most successful album ever – the only one in his 30-year plus career to have reached the Top 3 of the US charts.

Brown knew that he would sell out the show at the famous Apollo and, on 24 October 1962, he did just that; following the list of musicians on the album sleeve is a credit to '1,500 of the faithful at the Apollo Theater, 253 West 125th Street, Harlem, New York', who are vocal in their support.

The songs performed by Brown and his band included ten of his first 13 US R&B chart singles, many of which are still regarded as timeless classics, and which he was still performing in the '90s.

'Please, Please, Please', which is the opening song of a six and a half minute medley, also closes that medley, but was given a different title second time around, and one of the songs within the medley, 'Why Does Everything Happen To Me' was given the title of 'Strange Things Happen' on subsequent reissues of the album, as that was its title when it was a 1952 US R&B hit for Roy Hawkins, who co-wrote the song.

Brown was supported by The Famous Flames, his trio of background vocalists: Bobby Byrd (who also played organ on 'Lost Someone'), 'Baby' Lloyd Stallworth and Bobby Bennett.

ENTERTAINER EXTRAORDINAIRE

James Brown, 'The Godfather of Soul', celebrated his 100th hit in the US R&B chart in 1980. He continued to increase that figure to be rated the US's Top R&B performer, a title he may hold in perpetuity. No less than 58 of his hits had charted before 1970. His early work remains unequalled – The Who covered both 'Please, Please, Please' and 'I Don't Mind' on their debut album, and Brown was regarded by London's Mods as a hero; a complete edition of the popular TV show, 'Ready, Steady, Go!' was devoted to him when he toured the UK during the mid-'60s. Described at the start of this album by compere/pianist Lucas 'Fats' Gonder as 'the hardest working man in show business', James Brown has always lived up to that description, being an incredible dancer who is constantly on the move. His well-rehearsed routine, when he pretends to be exhausted at the climax of his show, is one of the most magical moments in rock.

THE FREEWHEELIN' BOB DYLAN

BOB DYLAN (1963)

Produced by John Hammond
Total running time: 50.09
Released in the US on Columbia Records and
in the UK on CBS Records

SIDE ONE
Blowin' In The Wind (Bob Dylan)
Girl From The North Country (Bob Dylan)
Masters Of War (Bob Dylan)
Down The Highway (Bob Dylan)
Bob Dylan's Blues (Bob Dylan)
A Hard Rain's A-Gonna Fall (Bob Dylan)

SIDE TWO
**Don't Think Twice, It's All Right
(Bob Dylan)**
Bob Dylan's Dream (Bob Dylan)
Oxford Town (Bob Dylan)
Talking World War III Blues (Bob Dylan)
**Corrina, Corrina
(Adapted & arranged by Bob Dylan)**
**Honey, Just Allow Me One More Chance
(Henry Thomas/Bob Dylan)**
I Shall Be Free (Bob Dylan)

T he second album by Dylan caused far greater waves than his eponymous debut. It sold considerably more copies, enough to almost take it into the US Top 20, and gave him his first gold album, a considerable achievement so early in his career. Most importantly, it signalled that the Woody Guthrie disciple from small-town Minnesota was Guthrie's equal as a songwriter, particularly of so called 'protest' songs.

The nuclear threat and war in general (with particular reference to the Cuban missile crisis of the previous autumn), and the ever-elusive concepts of freedom and justice (especially as applied to black people) were targets addressed by Dylan in such now-familiar songs as 'Blowin' In The Wind', 'Masters Of War' and 'A Hard Rain's A-Gonna Fall',

while 'Girl From The North Country' made it clear that Dylan could also write a fine love song.

'Blowin' In The Wind' was the only one of those songs where Dylan's tune was as original as his lyrics – the remainder all seem to be based on other songs: for example, 'Girl From The North Country' bears obvious similarities to 'Scarborough Fair'.

The chilling intensity of 'Blowin' In The Wind''s message was more easily digestible when performed by Peter, Paul & Mary, whose 1963 cover version made the US Top 3, while their follow-up hit, a version of 'Don't Think Twice It's All Right', was also a US Top 10 hit.

The message behind 'Hard Rain' made commercial success impossible in 1963. Ten years later, Bryan Ferry's cover was his first solo UK Top 10 hit.

DYLAN'S DREAM SESSIONS

Bob Dylan was signed to Columbia Records in 1961 by John Hammond (who had previously signed Bessie Smith and Billie Holiday) after working as a session musician on an album by Carolyn Hester that Hammond was producing. Hester recalled that when she had made her first album in Clovis, New Mexico, which was produced by Norman Petty (of Buddy Holly fame), her father had played harmonica. When she asked Hammond if she could use a harmonica player on the album he was producing, he agreed to the request, and asked whether she knew of someone suitable, whereupon she introduced her acquaintance from the Greenwich Village folk scene, Bob Dylan. Hammond was extremely impressed by the potential shown by the 20-year-old troubadour, and instantly offered him a recording contract of his own. Hester, who grew up in Texas, also recalled that Dylan was particularly pleased to play on her album because she had been a friend of Buddy Holly, who was one of his heroes.

A CHRISTMAS GIFT FOR YOU

PHIL SPECTOR (1963)

Produced by Phil Spector
Total running time: 35.14
Released in the US on Philles Records and in the UK on London Records

SIDE ONE

White Christmas (Berlin) (1)
Frosty The Snowman (Nelson/Rollins) (2)
The Bells Of St. Mary (Furber/Adams) (3)
Santa Claus Is Comin' To Town (Gillespie/Coots) (4)
Sleigh Ride (Parish/Anderson) (2)
(It's A) Marshmallow World (Sigman/De Rose) (1)

SIDE TWO

I Saw Mommy Kissing Santa Claus (Connor) (2)
Rudolph The Red-Nosed Reindeer (Marks) (4)
Winter Wonderland (Smith/Bernard) (1)
Parade Of The Wooden Soldiers (Jessel) (4)
Christmas (Baby Please Come Home)
(Spector/Greenwich/Barry) (1)
Here Comes Santa Claus
(Autry/Haldeman/Melka) (3)
Silent Night (Traditional) (5)

ARTISTS

(1) Darlene Love, (2) The Ronettes,
(3) Bob B. Soxx & The Blue Jeans,
(4) The Crystals,
(5) Phil Spector and Artists.

One of Phil Spector's greatest achievements as a record producer, this timeless album continues to attract attention every year, despite its advanced age.

Featuring the major acts signed to Spector's Philles label at the time, one of the unique points about this Christmas album is that its major star, Spector himself, hardly appears on the record as an artist – a short spoken dedication during 'Silent Night' is all we get.

What's more, his name only appeared in very small print at the bottom of the album sleeve. Yet this was very much Spector's album, on which he used the artists he had discovered to present a collection of seasonal novelties, pop standards and one original song in a modern musical style aimed at the young.

Artistically, it was a total success, but fate, in the shape of the death of US President John F. Kennedy, intervened. When he was shot in Dallas in November 1963, this album had just been released. The murder sent the US into shock, and there wasn't much music played on the radio that wasn't solemn – even the year's Christmas Number 1, 'Dominique' by Soeur Sourire (The Singing Nun), was quasi-religious.

Phil Spector continued to produce classic hits, such as 'You've Lost That Lovin' Feelin'' by The Righteous Brothers, but he never again attempted an album like this one. It remains the best ever Christmas album.

SOUND BACKING

Of the four acts featured on the album, The Crystals and The Ronettes were the biggest names. The black all-girl quartet The Crystals had accumulated six US Top 20 hits in under two years, including the chart-topping 'He's A Rebel' (written by Gene Pitney), although after this album, their success evaporated. Many lay the blame at Spector's door, because he was far more interested in his new discoveries, The Ronettes, whose lead vocalist, Ronnie (Veronica) Bennett, later became his wife.

The Ronettes were never as successful as The Crystals in hit terms, although 'Baby, I Love You', '(The Best Part Of) Breaking Up' and 'Walking In The Rain' are at least the equal of the biggest Crystals hits. Bob B. Soxx & The Blue Jeans featured lead vocalist Bobby Sheen, who had recorded a flop single for Spector in 1962, before the latter teamed him with Darlene Love and Fanita James to create his memorable US Top 10 hit 'Zip-A-Dee-Doo-Dah'. Darlene Love was also signed to Spector as a solo artist, and scored three medium-sized US hits in 1963.

WITH THE BEATLES

THE BEATLES (1963)

SIDE ONE
It Won't Be Long (Lennon/McCartney)
All I've Got To Do (Lennon/McCartney)
All My Loving (Lennon/McCartney)
Don't Bother Me (Harrison)
Little Child (Lennon/McCartney)
Till There Was You (Willson)
Please Mister Postman
(Dobbin/Garrett/Garman/Brianbert)

SIDE TWO
Roll Over Beethoven (Berry)
Hold Me Tight (Lennon/McCartney)
You Really Got A Hold On Me (Robinson)
I Wanna Be Your Man (Lennon/McCartney)
Devil In Her Heart (Drapkin)
Not A Second Time (Lennon/McCartney)
Money (Bradford/Gordy)

Produced by George Martin
Total running time: 33.26
Released in the UK by Parlophone Records and in the US by Capitol Records

R iding on an unprecedented wave of success in the UK, with three huge hit singles during the year ('Please Please Me', 'From Me To You' and 'She Loves You') along with the previous *Please Please Me* album's 30 chart-topping weeks, *With The Beatles* was a guaranteed Number 1 hit.

Soon after release, it displaced *Please Please Me* at the top of the UK chart, where it remained for 21 weeks. The quartet's love of Motown music is plain – Barrett Strong's 'Money' had been one of the first Motown hits (and was also included on the first EP by The Rolling Stones in early 1964); 'Please Mr. Postman' by The Marvelettes had been Motown's first US Number 1; and 'You Really Got A Hold On Me' was a US Top 10 hit for The Miracles at the start of 1963. Of the other cover versions, the Chuck Berry classic, 'Roll Over

Beethoven', was sung here by George Harrison; 'Till There Was You' was from a 1957 stage musical, 'The Music Man' (and was a million seller in the US in 1960 for Anita Bryant); and 'Devil In Her Heart' was an obscure 1962 non-hit by US group The Donays.

While none of the tracks on the LP were UK singles at the time, both 'All My Loving' and 'Roll Over Beethoven' were minor US hits.

'I Wanna Be Your Man' had been released as a UK single by The Rolling Stones, becoming their first Top 20 hit, and lead vocalist on the version by The Beatles was drummer Ringo Starr. The song 'Not A Second Time' is not one of the group's most widely-known compositions, but William Mann, music critic of The Times, likened the Aeolian cadences at the end of the song to Gustav Mahler's 'Song Of The Earth' – presumably meaning it as a compliment.

TRANSATLANTIC DIFFERENCES

The US version of this album was The Beatles' debut album in the US. Titled Meet The Beatles, it topped the US chart for 11 weeks, after having been released at the start of 1964, a few weeks before the group's arrival for the first time in the US and their television debut on 'The Ed Sullivan Show', in front of an estimated 73 million viewers. Meet The Beatles included the eight songs on With The Beatles written by members of the group and 'Till There Was You', but omitted five of the six cover versions, which were replaced by three Lennon/McCartney songs: 'I Want To Hold Your Hand', 'I Saw Her Standing There' and 'This Boy'.

The five tracks from With The Beatles omitted from Meet The Beatles along with assorted tracks from singles and EPs, were included on The Beatles' Second Album, which topped the US chart for five weeks, replacing Meet The Beatles at Number 1.

JOAN BAEZ IN CONCERT PART 2

JOAN BAEZ (1963)

SIDE ONE
Once I Had A Sweetheart (Traditional)
Jackaroe (Traditional)
Don't Think Twice, It's All Right (Bob Dylan)
We Shall Overcome
(Horton/Hamilton/Carawan/Seeger)
Portland Town (Adams)
Queen Of Hearts (Traditional)
Manha De Carnaval/Te Ador (Maria/Bonfa)

SIDE TWO
Long Black Veil (Wilkin/Dill)
Fennario (Traditional)
'Nu Bello Cardillo (Traditional)
With God On Our Side (Bob Dylan)
Three Fishers (Kingsley/Hullah)
Hush Little Baby (uncredited)
Battle Hymn Of The Republic
(Julia Ward Howe)

Producer not credited
Total running time: 46.58
Released in the US by Vanguard Records and in the UK by Fontana Records

Joan Baez's ethereal voice, as exemplified on this live album, made her a giant of the folk revival of the early '60s. This was particularly due to her major involvement with the civil rights movement, whose followers regarded the version of 'We Shall Overcome' included here (which was also her first US chart single) and which was recorded at Miles College, Birmingham, Alabama, as its anthem. It is the only track on the album with a specific recording location, no doubt because it became so celebrated. In April 1963, there were serious race riots in Alabama over the state's refusal to enforce anti-segregation laws and hundreds of people sang 'We Shall Overcome' as the riot unfolded.

Born in New York to a Mexican father and an English mother, Joan Baez began her all-consuming interest in politics while studying drama at university in Boston, Massachusetts, and began playing folk music, singing to her own acoustic guitar backing, at around the same time.

In 1960, she signed with leading folk label Vanguard, with whom she remained until 1971, initially using exclusively traditional material, but leavening it with contemporary songs after she became involved romantically with Bob Dylan, whose songs she performed and recorded.

This album not only achieved her highest ever US chart position, but was also her first LP to reach the UK chart.

DEFIANT DAYS

Joan Baez reached the US chart with 11 albums during the '60s, but after 1965 their success gradually decreased. In that year, she had founded The Institute For The Study Of Non-Violence in Carmel, California, after she and Donovan had led a protest march against the Vietnam war in London a few weeks before. In 1964, she had withheld 60% of her income tax due to the US Government in protest against the latter's expenditure on weaponry.

For much of the rest of the decade, she concentrated more on political protests than on her singing career. She was arrested in Oakland, California, in 1966, with over a hundred others for blocking the entrance to an Armed Forces Induction Centre, and was inside for ten days. In 1968, she married a draft dodger, David Harris, although he spent half their brief married life in prison because he was so determined not to be drafted. Baez's 1969 LP was titled David's Album and was dedicated to her husband whom she divorced not long after he was released from prison in 1971.

Joan Baez is the possessor of an exceptional voice which she continues to use to good effect in the '90s. However, her preoccupation with political matters has often tended to overshadow her music.

THE TIMES THEY ARE A-CHANGIN'

BOB DYLAN (1964)

SIDE ONE
The Times They Are A-Changin' (Bob Dylan)
Ballad Of Hollis Brown (Bob Dylan)
With God On Our Side (Bob Dylan)
One Too Many Mornings (Bob Dylan)
North Country Blues (Bob Dylan)

SIDE TWO
Only A Pawn In Their Game (Bob Dylan)
Boots Of Spanish Leather (Bob Dylan)
When The Ship Comes In (Bob Dylan)
The Lonesome Death Of Hattie Carroll (Bob Dylan)
Restless Farewell (Bob Dylan)

Produced by Tom Wilson
Total running time: 45.35

Released in the US on Columbia Records and in the UK on CBS Records.

The runaway success of the previous year's *Freewheelin'* album had made Bob Dylan a star, and he wasn't about to change his successful approach for its follow-up. However, *The Times They Are A-Changin'* was far more accurately focussed on its targets than the earlier album's slingshot attack on war, racial prejudice and inequality.

This third Dylan album produced fewer cover versions, but at least as much controversy, not least because its songs dealt with more specific topics: 'Hollis Brown' was the true story of a farmer from South Dakota whose economic plight led him to kill his wife and five children before committing suicide, while 'Only A Pawn' tells the story of the murder of black civil rights activist Medgar Evers. 'Hattie Carroll' was another real person, a 51-year-old black woman with ten children, who was murdered by a rich boy. This sentence after being found guilty of the crime was a prison term of only six months.

The title track was a clarion call to the burgeoning international protest movement, while the ironic 'With God On Our Side' (also recorded by British group, Manfred Mann, featuring Paul Jones as vocalist) was an exceptionally bitter indictment of hypocrisy mainly aimed at politicians and racists.

Perhaps due to its anti-establishment antagonism, the album peaked higher in the US than *Freewheelin'*, but didn't equal the latter's gold status.

PRODUCTION PROBLEMS

Having been largely advised by producer John Hammond since 1962, by this time Dylan had acquired a manager, Albert Grossman, who immediately tried to re-negotiate Dylan's contract with Columbia. Hammond reacted to this unwelcome (and unsuccessful) pressure by appointing another producer, Tom Wilson, a young black A&R man, who went on to produce Dylan's next two albums, Another Side Of Bob Dylan and Bringing It All Back Home. Despite including several songs which became hits when they were covered, Another Side Of Bob Dylan peaked outside the US Top 40.

On a 1964 concert tour of Britain, promoting The Times They Are A-Changin', Dylan met several British rock luminaries of the time, such as The Rolling Stones and The Beatles, whom he allegedly introduced to the magic of marijuana. Later that year, he returned to the UK for a second tour, this time accompanied by a film crew, to promote Another Side Of Bob Dylan. The resulting footage became the celebrated 'Don't Look Back', one of the most acclaimed rock documentaries ever made. Dylan's romantic life also changed in 1964 – having split up from his previous girlfriend, Suze Rotolo (pictured with Dylan on the sleeve of Freewheelin'), he had been introduced to Sara Lowndes, who became his wife.

THE ROLLING STONES

THE ROLLING STONES (1964)

SIDE ONE
(Get Your Kicks On) Route 66 (Troup)
I Just Want To Make Love To You (Dixon)
Honest I Do (Reed)
I Need You Baby (Mona) (McDaniels)
Now I've Got A Witness (Like Uncle Phil And Uncle Gene) (Phelge)
Little By Little (Phelge/Spector)

SIDE TWO
I'm A King Bee (Moore)
Carol (Berry)
Tell Me (You're Coming Back) (Jagger/Richards)
Can I Get A Witness (Holland/Dozier/Holland)
You Can Make It If You Try (Jarrett)
Walking The Dog (Thomas)

Produced by Andrew Loog Oldham/Eric Easton
Total running time: 32.32
Released in the UK on Decca Records and in the US on London Records

T he first reaction of London fans was that too many onstage favourites were missing from this debut LP. In hindsight, it perfectly captured the excitement The Rolling Stones created as they played to packed audiences at the Crawdaddy Club, Richmond.

A week after its release, it replaced *With The Beatles* at the top of the UK chart, where it remained for 12 weeks until the arrival of *A Hard Day's Night*.

It also omitted the first three hit singles: 'Come On', 'I Wanna Be Your Man' and 'Not Fade Away'. But the Buddy Holly B-side was on the US version, instead of the repetitive Bo Diddley item.

The Chuck Berry connection was acknowledged with 'Route 66' and 'Carol', as was blues and Motown, so the past and present were well in hand.

More intriguing was the future – the album featured three group originals, one under the alias Phelge ('Little By Little', the B-side of the 'Not Fade Away' single). It was co-written with Phil Spector, who played maracas on the track. 'Little By Little' also featured Gene Pitney, who had just charted with a Jagger/Richards song, 'That Girl Belongs To Yesterday', on piano.

The ballad 'Tell Me' was the first Rolling Stones record with a Jagger/Richards songwriting credit.

Ian Stewart played keyboards on four tracks, despite no longer being a group member – manager/producer Oldham disliked his 'straight' image.

ROLLING ON

Four of the five group members on The Stones' debut album remained with the band until January 1993, when bass player Bill Wyman (who was by then not far away from his 60th birthday!), decided that there had to be more to life at his age than touring and recording with 'the greatest rock'n'roll band in the world', as they were once described.

Vocalist/group leader Mick Jagger is still one of the best-known icons of the '60s, marginally ahead of guitarist Keith Richards, his songwriting partner of 30 years.

Charlie Watts rarely says much to the media, but remains one of the most reliable drummers in rock history. The fifth member of the group's line-up on this album, Brian Jones, died in 1969 in mysterious circumstances.

The Stones took a little longer than The Beatles to break into the national consciousness. Two albums behind the Fab Four when this LP was released, they were able to benefit from the Liverpool quartet's pioneering work in the US.

One of the most interesting things about this album is that it is the only one of the group's first six albums to have been reissued on compact disc in exactly the same form as the original UK vinyl version.

A HARD DAY'S NIGHT

THE BEATLES (1964)

SIDE ONE
A Hard Day's Night (Lennon/McCartney)
I Should Have Known Better
(Lennon/McCartney)
If I Fell (Lennon/McCartney)
I'm Happy Just To Dance With You
(Lennon/McCartney)
And I Love Her (Lennon/McCartney)
Tell Me Why (Lennon/McCartney)
Can't Buy Me Love (Lennon/McCartney)

SIDE TWO
Any Time At All (Lennon/McCartney)
I'll Cry Instead (Lennon/McCartney)
Things We Said Today (Lennon/McCartney)
When I Get Home (Lennon/McCartney)
You Can't Do That (Lennon/McCartney)
I'll Be Back (Lennon/McCartney)

Produced by George Martin
Total running time: 30.32
Released in the UK by Parlophone Records and in the US by Capitol Records

ith the massive commercial success of their first two albums and four singles, all within a year, it was an obvious move for The Beatles to star in their own feature films. *A Hard Day's Night* was the first.

This is not precisely the soundtrack album: only the songs on the first side were featured in the movie, while the tracks on side two were recorded specifically for this album (apart from 'I'll Cry Instead', which was scheduled for inclusion in the film, but finally deemed unsuitable by director Richard Lester). That track was included on the original US album, which omitted the other tracks on the second side of the UK album, but included four instrumental versions of Beatles songs arranged by George Martin and played by an orchestra.

Those tracks, along with all of those on the first side and 'I'll Cry Instead', made up the third Beatles LP released by Capitol in the US, *Something New*.

Something New remained at Number 1 for 14 weeks. *A Hard Day's Night* topped the UK chart for 21 successive weeks from July to December 1964.

Before the album was released, both 'Can't Buy Me Love' and the title track had been released as singles which went to Number 1 on both sides of the Atlantic, so its success was pre-ordained.

The album gave several other artists material — there had been over 350 versions of 'And I Love Her' by 1972. Two covers of the title song were hits, one a monologue by Peter Sellers in the style of Sir Laurence Olivier's cinematic King Richard III, the other a jazz instrumental by The Ramsey Lewis Trio.

MOVING MOVIES IN NEW DIRECTIONS

American film director Richard Lester launched an entirely new style of pop movies with 'A Hard Day's Night'. Lester had first attracted attention in 1959 by directing a legendary short movie, 'The Running, Jumping & Standing Still Film', starring Spike Milligan and Peter Sellers, who later recorded the title songs of both the first two feature films starring The Beatles. Lester also directed the group's second feature film, 'Help!', in 1965, which was filmed in colour rather than the black and white used for 'A Hard Day's Night'. One of the minor parts in the earlier film was played by Patti Boyd, a noted model, who later became Mrs. George Harrison and, more recently, Mrs. Eric Clapton. Among the other stars of 'A Hard Day's Night' were three noted comic actors, Wilfred Brambell, who achieved fame in the long-running TV series, 'Steptoe And Son', Deryck Guyler and Victor Spinetti. The film was the subject of a Royal World Premiere on 6 July 1964, in London, with HRH Princess Margaret and her husband, Lord Snowdon, as guests of honour. Its US premiere took place in New York on 12 August 1964.

I WALK THE LINE

JOHNNY CASH (1964)

SIDE ONE
I Walk The Line (Cash)
Bad News (Loudermilk)
Folsom Prison Blues (Cash)
Give My Love To Rose (Cash)
Hey Porter (Cash)
I Still Miss Someone (Cash/Cash Jnr.)

SIDE TWO
Understand Your Man (Cash)
Wreck Of The Old 97
(Arr. Cash/Johnson/Blake)
Still In Town (Cochran/Howard)
Big River (Cash)
Goodbye, Little Darlin' Goodbye
(Marvin/Autry)
Troublesome Waters
(M. Carter/E. H. Carter/Deen)

Produced by Don Law & Frank Jones
Total running time: 34.02
Released in the US by Columbia Records and in the UK by CBS Records

This album, the second by Cash to achieve gold status, includes re-recordings of six tracks which he had previously cut for Sun: 'I Walk The Line', 'Hey Porter', 'Wreck Of The Old 97', 'Big River', 'Folsom Prison Blues' and 'Give My Love To Rose'. It was the perfect showcase for his inimitable, gravelly voice, a voice dripping with experience.

The idea appeared to be to re-launch Cash's flagging career, which had been at a low ebb in the early '60s, when constant touring had made him reliant on drugs and alcohol – and that, in its turn, had alienated him from his family.

In 1963, he had recorded 'Ring Of Fire', a song co-written by June Carter (of the Carter Family, a legendary country act), which became his first US Top 20 hit since 1958. It was a temporary reprieve, and Cash, who had become deeply addicted to amphetamines, spent a drug-crazed (by his own admission) year and a half with a similarly wired Waylon Jennings.

Benefitting from the success of 'Ring Of Fire', one of the new tracks from this LP, 'Understand Your Man', was a US Top 40 hit. In 1967, Carter not only helped cure Cash of his drug habit, but introduced him to fundamentalist Christianity, and the couple were married in 1968.

With several hit songs (albeit re-recordings), this album resembled a 'Greatest Hits' package, and was his last original LP to achieve gold status for four years.

INSIDE JOBS

While 'I Walk The Line' had been his first US Top 20 pop hit in 1956, the preceding single by Cash, 'Folsom Prison Blues', had also been very popular that year and became even more so in 1968, when Cash recorded a million-selling live album at the notoriously tough penal institution. Cash had first played in a prison in 1960, when he performed at San Quentin – among his literally captive audience there was Merle Haggard, who was so inspired by Cash's example that he turned his back on crime after serving his sentence (for burglary) and became an internationally famous country star himself. Cash returned to San Quentin in 1969, and a TV documentary of his concert there was filmed and recorded.

Released as another live album, Johnny Cash At San Quentin outdid Johnny Cash At Folsom Prison by topping the US album chart for a month and becoming his most successful album ever. His status with rock fans considerably improved when he became friendly with Bob Dylan, with whom he duetted on 'Girl From The North Country' on the latter's Nashville Skyline album in 1969. Still on the road in the '90s, Johnny Cash remains a household name and arguably the ultimate international star of country music.

ALL SUMMER LONG

THE BEACH BOYS (1964)

Produced by Brian Wilson
Total running time: 24.04
Released in the US & the UK by Capitol Records

SIDE ONE
I Get Around (B. Wilson)
All Summer Long (B. Wilson)
Hushabye (D. Pomus/M. Shuman)
Little Honda (B. Wilson/M. Love)
We'll Run Away (B. Wilson/G. Usher)
Carl's Big Chance (B. Wilson/C. Wilson)

SIDE TWO
Wendy (B. Wilson)
Do You Remember? (B. Wilson)
Girls On The Beach (B. Wilson/M. Love)
Drive In (B. Wilson)
Our Favourite Recording Sessions
(B. Wilson/D. Wilson/C. Wilson/
M. Love/A. Jardine)
Don't Back Down (B. Wilson)

The last album to be inspired by Beach Boys leader/ songwriter/producer Brian Wilson before his nervous breakdown provides suitable testimony to his ability to arrange fine harmonies.

The first Beach Boys LP on Capitol had been released at the end of 1962, and *All Summer Long* was their sixth album in under two years, accounting for the pitifully short playing time here.

However, it did include the group's first million-selling single, 'I Get Around', which topped the US chart as well as two more US hit singles, 'Wendy' and 'Little Honda'. Their fourth US Top 10 LP in 18 months, it failed to chart in the UK.

After the release of *All Summer Long*, Brian Wilson gave up touring with the band. In late 1964, four months after its release, he suffered a nervous breakdown caused by pressure of work (and also involving his hearing – he is virtually deaf in one ear). From that point on, he rarely appeared with the group onstage. The title track of this album was heard over the closing credits of the movie, 'American Graffiti', while 'Little Honda' was covered by The Hondells (another Californian band working along similar musical lines).

'Hushabye', a cover of a 1959 US Top 20 hit by The Mystics, a New York doo-wop quintet, reflects Wilson's love of vocal harmonies, and 'Carl's Big Chance', featuring Brian's younger brother, Carl Wilson, on lead guitar, was the last surf-styled instrumental the group recorded.

FAMILY FUN

The Beach Boys played their first concert under that name on New Year's Eve, 1961, with a line-up of Brian Wilson (vocals, bass, keyboards), his brothers Dennis (vocals, drums) and Carl (vocals, lead guitar), their cousin Mike Love (vocals) and schoolfriend Al Jardine (vocals, guitar).

They had previously played together at school functions under the name Carl & The Passions and The Pendletones, but adopted the name of The Beach Boys as their debut single was titled 'Surfin''.

In early 1962, Jardine left the group for 18 months to study dentistry, and was replaced for that period by David Marks, who lived across the street from the Wilson family in Hawthorne, a suburb of Los Angeles. Signing with Capitol in 1962, the group scored an immediate hit single with 'Surfin' Safari'/'409', both sides of which reached the US chart, and at the end of the year, their debut album, also titled Surfin' Safari, reached the US Top 40. The following year brought three US Top 10 albums, Surfin' USA, Surfer Girl and Little Deuce Coupe. The first two went gold, the last achieved platinum status.

This was incredible success for a group whose ages in 1963 ranged between 16 (Carl Wilson) and 22 (Mike Love).

ANIMAL TRACKS

THE ANIMALS (1965)

SIDE ONE
Mess Around (Nugetre)
How You've Changed (Berry)
Hallelujah I Love Her So (Charles)
I Believe To My Soul (Charles)
Worried Life Blues (Merriweather)
Roberta (Smith)

SIDE TWO
I Ain't Got You (Arnold)
Bright Lights Big City (Reed)
Let The Good Times Roll (Lee)
For Miss Caulker (Burdon)
Roadrunner (McDaniel)

Produced by Mickie Most
Total running time: 31.54
Released in the UK by Columbia/EMI Records and in the US by MGM Records

The second album by the R&B quintet from Newcastle, *Animal Tracks* sounds as unpretentiously excellent today as it did nearly 30 years ago.

Eric Burdon & Co tipped their hats to all the right American R&B heroes – Chuck Berry, Ray Charles, Jimmy Reed and Bo Diddley. They also added covers from more obscure acts like Shirley & Lee. Unlike The Beatles, they did not dominate the album with their own material.

Singer Burdon and organist Alan Price led from the front. A reliable backbone was provided by a fairly anonymous guitar/bass/drums trio. With one of the more memorable sleeves of the era, *Animal Tracks* was an album of which The Animals could be justifiably proud.

The US title of the album was *The Animals On Tour* (suggesting incorrectly that it was a live album), and it omitted 'Roberta' and 'For Miss Caulker' (both would later appear on the group's third US LP, titled *Animal Tracks* but, confusingly, with an entirely different track listing from the UK-originated *Animal Tracks*) and 'Roadrunner'.

The LP only included one track which was issued as a 45, vocalist Eric Burdon's 'For Miss Caulker', and spent six months in the UK chart, peaking in the Top 10.

In the US, things were very different. After their chart-topping debut with 'House Of The Rising Sun', the group's hits had been small, and interest was so limited that *The Animals On Tour* only just got to the Top 100.

THE PRICE OF SUCCESS

Formed in 1962 as The Alan Price Combo, when vocalist Eric Burdon joined The Alan Price Trio (Price on keyboards, Bryan 'Chas' Chandler on bass and John Steel on drums), the group became a quintet when guitarist Hilton Valentine was invited to join. Renamed The Animals (apparently due to their wild stage act), the group became local stars in the North-East before a two-month stint in Hamburg in 1963. In 1964 they moved to London, signing with independent record producer Mickie Most, who had seen them, only weeks before, when he visited Newcastle, playing on a package tour starring The Everly Brothers and Bo Diddley, and with The Rolling Stones as bottom of the bill opening act. In 18 months they recorded around 40 tracks together.

A significant personnel change occurred when Price left the group. By late 1966, Burdon, the only remaining original member, led a new group, Eric Burdon & The Animals, concentrating on the US market with reasonable success until the end of 1968, when they fell apart. Price enjoyed six UK hit singles as leader of The Alan Price Set between 1966 and 1968.

BRINGING IT ALL BACK HOME

BOB DYLAN (1965)

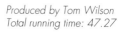

SIDE ONE
Subterranean Homesick Blues (Dylan)
She Belongs To Me (Dylan)
Maggie's Farm (Dylan)
Love Minus Zero/No Limit (Dylan)
Outlaw Blues (Dylan)
On The Road Again (Dylan)
Bob Dylan's 115th Dream (Dylan)

SIDE TWO
Mr. Tambourine Man (Dylan)
Gates Of Eden (Dylan)
It's Alright Ma (I'm Only Bleeding) (Dylan)
It's All Over Now, Baby Blue (Dylan)

Produced by Tom Wilson
Total running time: 47.27

Released in the US on Columbia Records and in the UK on CBS Records

Dylan's fifth album was his biggest yet, becoming his second to go gold and his first to make the US Top 10. For the first time, rock musicians played on a Dylan album, which broadened his audience while also allowing him to return to his rock'n'roll roots – his stated ambition in a High School Yearbook had been 'to follow Little Richard' and his first musical job of any note was a brief spell as a pianist in Bobby Vee's backing band, from which he was fired.

Certainly, the opening 'Subterranean Homesick Blues' was very different from what had gone before – a fusillade of lyrics above a Chuck Berry-styled electric rock backing, with lines such as the one about not following leaders (very Dylanesque) and watching parking meters (good advice). It was his first US Top 40 single and his second UK Top 10 hit in four weeks.

British singles-buyers latched on to Dylan before their US counterparts, and 'Maggie's Farm' almost made the UK Top 20 a few weeks later.

During the '80s, when Margaret Thatcher was Prime Minister of Britain, 'Maggie's Farm' became an anti-Thatcher anthem and, like a number of the songs here, has frequently been covered. Rick Nelson's first US hit single since 1965 came in 1969 with his version of 'She Belongs To Me', while 'Love Minus Zero', 'Gates Of Eden', and 'It's Alright Ma' have all been covered by credible artists, as has 'It's All Over Now, Baby Blue' (recorded by Joan Baez, The Grateful Dead, Leon Russell and others).

The album's most familiar song is 'Mr. Tambourine Man'. It was a worldwide hit for The Byrds, who recorded several songs from *Bringing It All Back Home*, an album that has rarely been equalled as a source of hits.

AN ELECTRIC RECEPTION

No musician's credits appear on Bringing It All Back Home, *but Dylan's backing band is likely to have included guitarist Mike Bloomfield of the Paul Butterfield Blues Band, and it seems probable that other members of that band, including R&B harmonica virtuoso Butterfield himself, also played on the electric rock tracks.*

There was considerable controversy when Dylan played at the Newport Folk Festival in July 1965, backed by the Butterfield Band and organist Al Kooper, then a member of New York's critically acclaimed Blues Project. Some members of the audience had not expected this loud music, and it was made clear by several legendary members of the folk aristocracy (notably Pete Seeger, who reputedly called Dylan 'Judas'!) that they felt betrayed by what they regarded as this heavy-handed approach. Perhaps they failed to recognise that Dylan needed to press forward and reach a wider audience (which this album had achieved), and that to play acoustically would not allow him to accurately represent himself.

THEM

THEM (1965)

Produced by Tommy Scott except * by Bert Berns and ** by Dick Rowe
Total running time: 39.37
Released in the UK on Decca Records and in the US on Parrot Records

SIDE ONE
Mystic Eyes (Morrison)
If You And I Could Be As Two (Morrison)
Little Girl (Morrison)
Just A Little Bit (Gordon)
*I Gave My Love A Diamond (Berns) ***
*Gloria (Morrison) ****
You Just Can't Win (Morrison)

SIDE TWO
*Go On Home, Baby (Berns) ***
Don't Look Back (Hooker)
I Like It Like That (Morrison)
I'm Gonna Dress In Black (Gillon)
Bright Lights Big City (Reed)
*My Little Baby (Berns/Farrell) ***
(Get Your Kicks On) Route 66 (Troup)

his debut album captured the energetic approach that made Them the first Irish act of modern times to make an international impact.

Even though he was only 18 years old when he formed the group in Belfast in late 1963, vocalist Van Morrison was master of his own destiny. During his two years fronting the band, the only other ever-present member of Them was bass player Alan Henderson, with a dozen different musicians filling the other three positions, including five drummers.

After signing with Decca Records in London in mid-1964, they recorded an excellent version of the Big Joe Williams classic, 'Baby Please Don't Go', which was a UK Top 10 hit in early 1965 and was used as the signature tune of the 'Ready Steady Go' TV series. A Morrison original, 'Gloria', was its B-side and the group's first US hit single.

Now a chart act, Them swiftly went into the studio to record enough tracks for their debut album. It consisted of a few R&B classics written by blues greats such as John Lee Hooker and Jimmy Reed, plus three songs by Bert Berns, the American producer who had been brought in to boost the group's chances of a second hit.

He achieved that with 'Here Comes The Night', included on the US version of the album), and several songs by Van, which are highly interesting, especially 'Mystic Eyes'.

MAIN MAN VAN

One of the perceived reasons for the continual personnel changes within Them almost certainly stemmed from the fact that few of the group members, other than Morrison, were allowed to play on recording sessions. Their places were taken by session men so there is considerable doubt about which group members backed Morrison on this album.

It was overshadowed by the first two albums by their Decca stablemates, The Rolling Stones, regarded by the label as a much higher priority. By the time of their second album, Them Again, released in early 1966 (only eight months after this debut), the group was starting to fall apart. In mid-1966 Morrison left for the US, where a cover version of 'Gloria' by Chicago garage band The Shadows of Knight had reached the Top 10.

After contacting Bert Berns, whom he felt to be Them's only worthwhile producer, Morrison signed with Bang Records, the label Berns owned in New York, and in 1967 'Brown Eyed Girl' became his first solo US Top 10 single. However, he was indignant when Berns released Blowin' Your Mind, an album Morrison claimed was mainly unfinished demos. The sudden death of Bert Berns of a heart attack in late 1967 compelled Morrison to find a new label, and the first result was the stunning Astral Weeks.

HIGHWAY 61 REVISITED

BOB DYLAN (1965)

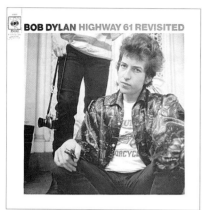

SIDE ONE
Like A Rolling Stone (Bob Dylan) *
Tombstone Blues (Bob Dylan)
**It Takes A Lot To Laugh, It Takes A Train
To Cry (Bob Dylan)**
From A Buick 6 (Bob Dylan)
Ballad Of A Thin Man (Bob Dylan)

SIDE TWO
Queen Jane Approximately (Bob Dylan)
Highway 61 Revisited (Bob Dylan)
Just Like Tom Thumb's Blues (Bob Dylan)
Desolation Row (Bob Dylan)

*Produced by Bob Johnston except ***
produced by Tom Wilson
Total running time: 51.39
*Released in the US by Columbia Records
and in the UK by CBS Records*

A milestone in Bob Dylan's career, this magnificent classic was his first fully electric album after the transitional *Bringing It All Back Home.*

Introduced by the amazing (six minutes long and still a Top 5 single on both sides of the Atlantic) 'Like A Rolling Stone', featuring Al Kooper's hypnotic swirling organ, this is a special album: a stunning collection of songs.

Some of these songs are bitingly accurate in their universal realism, although many have been misread, like 'Ballad Of A Thin Man', the anti-authority protest – who is it aimed at? The establishment, or as one biographer suggests, at Dylan himself? It may not matter much, as the general sound of this album makes it undeniably impressive, from the million-selling hit single via the trucking title track about the road which runs from top to bottom of the US, to the staggering 11-minutes-plus 'Desolation Row' with its endless stream of imagery: mentions are made of Joan of Arc, the Hunchback of Notre Dame, the Good Samaritan, Noah, Einstein, Robin Hood, the Phantom of The Opera, Casanova, and two poets, Ezra Pound (an American) and T.S. Eliot (a Briton), although quite why they're mentioned is something else entirely.

Even the titles of songs like 'Queen Jane Approximately' sound enticing, and Dylan has been quoted as saying that he rarely plans lyrical inclusions for their meaning, but more frequently because of the sound of the words. This produces fascinating verbal juxtapositions which fit neatly with Dylan's great performances of his songs.

HEADY DAYS

On 22 November 1965, shortly after this album was released, Dylan married Sara Lowndes, although no public announcement of his nuptials was made until three months later. Almost immediately, he began a series of concert tours both in the US and in Europe, returning to the US between legs of the lengthy roadwork stint to record tracks for his next album at the Columbia/CBS studio in Nashville.

According to one source, it had been suggested that Dylan should record in Music City some time before, but the head of the label's country music division had vetoed the idea. Dylan was touring with Canadian group The Hawks (previously the backing band for veteran '50s rocker Ronnie Hawkins, and later renamed The Band), but recording in Nashville with seasoned and in-demand session musicians who had made the Tennessee city a hit factory. His work was inspired.

Song after brilliant song spilled out of his speeding mind, and many of his contemporary live concerts remain legendary, such as his celebrated Royal Albert Hall appearance in May 1966. Recorded for a live album, a quarter of a century later it had still not been officially released, although tens of thousands of Dylan fans all over the world owned bootleg recordings.

OTIS BLUE

OTIS REDDING (1965)

SIDE ONE
Ole Man Trouble (Otis Redding)
Respect (Otis Redding)
Change Gonna Come (Sam Cooke)
Down In The Valley (Solomon Burke)
I've Been Loving You Too Long
(Redding/Butler)

SIDE TWO
Shake (Sam Cooke)
My Girl (William Robinson/Ronald White)
Wonderful World (Barbara Campbell)
Rock Me Baby (B.B. King/Joe Josea)
Satisfaction (Mick Jagger/Keith Richard)
You Don't Miss Your Water (William Bell)

Produced by Jim Stewart
Total running time: 32.54
Released in the US on Volt Records and in the UK on Atlantic Records

tis Blue is without doubt the finest original soul/R&B album of the '60s and one of the all-time classics of the genre. This magnificent collection has lost none of its many brilliant qualities despite the passage of time.

It features cover versions of contemporary soul hits ('My Girl', the Smokey Robinson-penned US Number 1 for The Temptations; 'Down In The Valley', a 1962 hit for Solomon Burke; and the same year's 'You Don't Miss Your Water', by Redding's label-mate, William Bell) and no less than three songs associated with Sam Cooke.

While some of the cover versions do not improve on the originals, Otis's swooping vocal of 'Change Gonna Come' made this cover the best-remembered version.

Similarly, Mick Jagger must have known that 'Satisfaction' could never be his song exclusively after this Otis cover. Otis clearly had little interest in whether the writers of a song were black or white – if it was good, he could make it a masterpiece, even a chart-topper like 'My Girl' or 'Satisfaction'.

Ironically, two of his own compositions here were later covered with great success: 'Respect' by Aretha Franklin and 'I've Been Loving You Too Long' by Tina Turner.

While Jim Stewart is credited with 'supervision', engineer Tom Dowd noted that it was a 'Southern tradition never to individualise who made a record or how it was made'. Thus there are no musician credits on the sleeve, although Dowd's memory suggests that Booker T. & The MGs were probably involved.

MAKING IT FROM MACON

While Sam Cooke was an inspiration for Redding during the '60s, his first idol was Little Richard, born, like Redding, in Macon, Georgia. Redding initially copied Richard's vocal style. Success in local talent shows led to a position as vocalist (and apparently chauffeur to the boss) with Johnny Jenkins & The Pinetoppers. In the remaining studio time, following a Pinetoppers recording session, Redding cut his first US R&B hit, 'These Arms Of Mine', in 1963, after which he swiftly rose to international fame.

Sadly, he never knew that his biggest hit, '(Sittin' On) The Dock Of The Bay', would top the US chart, as he only recorded the song three days before his death in a plane crash on 10 December 1967, having emerged into the US spotlight at the start of the year after his dynamic performance at 'Monterey Pop', the first great rock festival.

Otis Redding accumulated 28 US pop chart hits, almost a third of them posthumously. We may never see his like again.

GOING TO A GO-GO

SMOKEY ROBINSON & THE MIRACLES (1965)

Produced by Bill 'Smokey' Robinson except
*, which was produced by Hal Davis &
Marc Gordon
Total running time: 33.41
Released on Tamla in the US and Tamla
Motown in the UK

SIDE ONE
The Tracks Of My Tears
(Moore/Robinson/Tarplin)
Going To A Go-Go
(Moore/Robinson/Rogers/Johnson)
Ooo Baby Baby (Moore/Robinson)
My Girl Has Gone
(Moore/Robinson/White/Tarplin)
In Case You Need Love (Robinson)
Choosey Beggar (Moore/Robinson)

SIDE TWO
Since You Won My Heart
(Robinson/Stevenson)
From Head To Toe (Robinson)
All That's Good (Moore/Robinson)
My Baby Changes Like The Weather
*(Davis/Wilson) ***
Let Me Have Some (Robinson/Rogers)
A Fork In The Road
(Moore/Robinson/White)

illiam 'Smokey' Robinson was
more than just a beautifully
soulful singer with a high
voice – he was a songwriter
admired by rock royalty. The songs on
this album show why.

This was The Miracles's most
successful original album by far,
reaching the US Top 10 during a chart
residency of over nine months. Unlike
many Motown albums of the time, it
included more than just a couple of hits
padded out with filler – the first four
tracks were all US Top 20 hits, while
'Choosey Beggar' was a Top 40 US
R&B hit. The title track was the group's
first UK hit single in 1966, while 'The
Tracks Of My Tears' became their first
UK Top 10 hit in 1969.

Robinson was lead vocalist,
songwriter and producer for The
Miracles and Bob Dylan called him
'today's greatest living American poet'.
The sensitivity displayed in the lyrics of
the songs on this album show why Dylan
was justified in making such a statement.

Robinson could easily sing, write and
produce songs brilliantly, as evidenced
by the sublime 'Tracks Of My Tears', the
yearning ballads, 'Ooo Baby Baby' and
'My Girl Has Gone', and the uptempo
'From Head To Toe' (later covered by
Elvis Costello and which actually wasn't
a hit for Smokey).

These songs sound as fresh today as
they did in those golden Motown days.

SMOKEY'S HITS

*Formed at a Detroit school in 1955
(when lead vocalist Robinson was
15 years old), the other longstanding
members of The Miracles were
Bobby Rogers (tenor), Ronnie White
(baritone) and Warren 'Pete' Moore
(bass). From 1958-64, Claudette
Rogers (Bobby's sister, who later
married Smokey) was also a
member. Marv Tarplin (guitar) led the
group's backing band and also
helped Robinson and the other group
members to write several classic hits.
With 34 US chart singles during the
'60s, the group rate highly in the list
of the most prolific hitmakers, but
perhaps because other acts from the
Motown stable had more
chart-topping hits, The Miracles were
undervalued by record buyers.*

*Smokey's own image was less
attention-grabbing than those of
Diana Ross in The Supremes or Levi
Stubbs in The Four Tops, the two
biggest Motown acts. At the start of
1967, the name of the group was
changed from simply The Miracles to
reflect that Smokey was its leader.*

*He went solo in 1972, and was
replaced by William Griffin. Neither
the group nor its erstwhile leader
were as successful apart as they had
been together although both had
subsequent Number 1s.*

RUBBER SOUL

THE BEATLES (1965)

SIDE ONE
Drive My Car (Lennon/McCartney)
Norwegian Wood (This Bird Has Flown)
(Lennon/McCartney)
You Won't See Me (Lennon/McCartney)
Nowhere Man (Lennon/McCartney)
Think For Yourself (Harrison)
The Word (Lennon/McCartney)
Michelle (Lennon/McCartney)

SIDE TWO
What Goes On (Lennon/McCartney/Starkey)
Girl (Lennon/McCartney)
I'm Looking Through You (Lennon/McCartney)
In My Life (Lennon/McCartney)
Wait (Lennon/McCartney)
If I Needed Someone (Harrison)
Run For Your Life (Lennon/McCartney)

Produced by George Martin
Total running time: 35.50
Released in the UK by Parlophone Records and in the US by Capitol Records

As the '60s progressed, US versions of identically-titled UK Beatle LPs began to include a majority of similar tracks. Despite that, the US version of *Rubber Soul* still omitted 'Drive My Car', 'Nowhere Man', 'If I Needed Someone' and 'What Goes On', but included 'I've Just Seen A Face' and 'It's Only Love', both from the UK version of the group's previous LP, *Help!*.

Rubber Soul was released a few days after the end of the final UK tour by The Beatles and swiftly raced to the top of the UK chart, where it remained for nine weeks, three weeks longer than its time at Number 1 in the US.

As testimony to their continuing influence on their contemporaries, and as usual with a new Beatles album, several of the songs were eagerly covered by other acts. Most in demand was 'Michelle', a ballad with some of its English lyrics translated into French.

Other notable covers were 'If I Needed Someone' by The Hollies (although George Harrison made it clear he disliked their version), and 'In My Life', the title track of a 1967 LP by Judy Collins which went gold.

'Nowhere Man' was written by John Lennon about his lonely life as a celebrity, while his 'Norwegian Wood' was about an illicit affair, and includes Harrison on sitar, the Indian instrument which soon afterwards also appeared on 'Paint It Black' by The Rolling Stones and Traffic's early hits.

'What Goes On' had Ringo Starr singing lead and Starr, the group's drummer, supposedly plays Hammond organ on 'I'm Looking Through You'.

CONTROVERSIAL AWARDS

One of the strangest things to happen to The Beatles in 1965 was the announcement that they had been awarded the MBE (Member of The Order Of The British Empire), which provoked a storm of protest. A former Canadian member of Parliament commented: 'The British house of royalty has put me on the same level as a bunch of numbskulls', which seemed a little excessive until John Lennon returned his MBE in 1969 as a protest against British involvement in a war in Africa, Britain's support of US policy in Vietnam, and because his single, 'Cold Turkey', was dropping down the charts.

HRH Queen Elizabeth II presented the MBEs in October at Buckingham Palace. The group later admitted to smoking a joint in the Palace's public toilet.

John Lennon's second book, 'A Spaniard In The Works', was published, following the previous year's 'In His Own Write'. The group also met one of their heroes, Elvis Presley, at his Californian home in Bel Air, where, so the story goes, Presley, Lennon & McCartney sang together informally.

THE PAUL BUTTERFIELD BLUES BAND

THE PAUL BUTTERFIELD BLUES BAND (1965)

SIDE ONE
Born In Chicago (Nick Gravenites)
Shake Your Money-Maker
(adpt. Butterfield)
Blues With A Feeling (W. Jacobs)
Thank You Mr. Poobah
(Butterfield/Bloomfield/Naftalin)
I Got My Mojo Working (Morganfield)
Mellow Down Easy (W. Dixon)

SIDE TWO
Screamin' (Bloomfield)
Our Love Is Drifting (Bishop/Butterfield)
Mystery Train (uncredited)
Last Night (W. Jacobs)
Look Over Yonders Wall (J. Clark)

Produced by Paul Rothchild
Total running time: 38.09
Released in the US & UK by Elektra Records

I f John Mayall was *the* British R&B pioneer in the '60s, his US equivalent was Chicago-born vocalist/harmonica star Paul Butterfield. This white 23-year-old led a band with a white front line and a black rhythm section who were as adept at playing the blues as any band in the world at that time.

Apart from Butterfield himself, a blues shouter correctly described in Pete Welding's authoritative sleeve note as 'his own man', not an impersonator, the band's other members were Mike Bloomfield on slide guitar, who earlier that year had played on Bob Dylan's 'Like A Rolling Stone', Elvin Bishop also on guitar, who went on to lead his own band in the mid-'70s, and Mark Naftalin (organ). Jerome Arnold (brother of noted bluesman Billy Boy Arnold) was on bass, and Sam Lay played drums (as well as taking lead vocal on the Muddy Waters epic, 'I Got My Mojo Working').

With seven of the 11 tracks from the classic Chicago blues repertoire – two by Little Walter Jacobs, a prime Butterfield harmonica influence, two from the Elmore James canon ('Shake Your Money-Maker' and 'Look Over Yonders Wall') and one each by Willie Dixon ('Mellow Down Easy') and Junior Parker ('Mystery Train') as well as 'Mojo', the band were clearly not confident about contemporary material. This was false modesty in the case of 'Born In Chicago', Butterfield's autobiographical song written by Nick Gravenites, another local white bluesman.

WHITE BLUES

Like John Mayall, Paul Butterfield frequently changed the personnel of his band. In both cases, there seems to have been a situation in which the leader was so good at discovering new stars that he eventually chose to replace them before he was forced to do so by their resignation.

Mike Bloomfield stayed for a second album with the Butterfield band, 1966's East West, their only LP to remain in the US chart for six months, before leaving for an intermittently successful solo career, among the highlights of which were Super Session with Al Kooper, and his own band, Electric Flag, which too often promised more than it delivered. When he left Butterfield, Elvin Bishop took over for the third album, The Resurrection of Pigboy Crabshaw (which was Bishop's nickname), but without Bloomfield, and even with the addition of a brass section, the band went into gradual decline, folding in 1971.

Apart from the seven US chart albums made by Butterfield and his ever-changing group before it finally disbanded, he also contributed to two other interesting '60s projects, a 1967 EP with John Mayall and his band, 'Bluesbreakers With Paul Butterfield', and five tracks on What's Shakin', a 1966 album featuring The Lovin' Spoonful, Tom Rush, Al Kooper and Eric Clapton & The Powerhouse, a studio band which included Jack Bruce and Steve Winwood.

DO YOU BELIEVE IN MAGIC?

THE LOVIN' SPOONFUL (1965)

Produced by Erik Jacobsen
Total running time: 30.23
Released in the US by Kama Sutra Records
and in the UK by Pye Records.

SIDE ONE
Do You Believe In Magic? (Sebastian)
Blues In The Bottle
(Sebastian/Yanovsky/Boone/
Butler/Stampfel/Weber)
Sportin' Life
(Sebastian/Yanovsky/Boone/Butler)
My Gal (Poor Gal)
(Sebastian/Yanovsky/Boone/
Butler/Kweskin/Jacobsen)
You Baby (Spector/Mann/Weill)
Fishin' Blues (Sebastian)

SIDE TWO
Did You Ever Have To Make Up Your Mind?
(Sebastian)
Wild About My Lovin' (Sebastian)
The Other Side Of This Life (Neil)
Younger Girl (Sebastian)

uite irresistible due equally to their group name and their contagious jug band sound, as exemplified on this album, this New York-based quartet rose to international fame with a dozen US hit singles. But within two and a half years the band had fallen apart.

Singer/songwriter John Sebastian (lead vocal, guitar, harmonica, autoharp) was well-known in the Greenwich Village folk scene, and the group's other major personality was lead guitarist/vocalist Zalman Yanovsky, a Canadian. Steve Boone (bass) and drummer Joe Butler completed the line-up. Sebastian and Yanovsky had met in The Mugwumps, whose other members, Cass Elliott and Denny Doherty, later helped to found The Mamas & Papas.

The group name was borrowed from a line in celebrated bluesman 'Mississippi' John Hurt's song, 'Coffee Blues' – 'I love my baby by the lovin' spoonful'. Their first single, a US Top 10 hit, 'Do You Believe In Magic?', was an instant classic, an affirmation of rock'n'roll music's qualities.

Kama Sutra's speed at following this hit resulted in their next single, 'You Didn't Have To Be So Nice', being from their second album. Its title track, 'Daydream', was their first US Top 3 single. The flip sides of each of these first three singles came from this debut album ('On The Road Again', 'My Gal' and 'Night Owl Blues'), and the A side of their fourth single (a second US Top 3 hit in three months!) was 'Did You Ever Have To Make Up Your Mind?'.

A SPOONFUL OF CELEBRITY

Initially regarded as New York's Beatles equivalent, The Lovin' Spoonful's virtually overnight rise from rehearsing at New York's Night Owl coffee house (which inspired 'Night Owl Blues') to international celebrity in well under a year, coupled with being by far the biggest act on their label, placed them under considerable pressure. In just over two years, they made four regular albums, as well as writing and recording two film soundtracks also released as albums. The watershed came when Yanovsky left the group – involved in a drug abuse case in late 1966, he was given the unenviable choice of being deported (as a Canadian) or becoming an informer. Sebastian was the only one of the four to achieve solo success, as the archetypal tie-dyed hippie of the 'Woodstock' festival and feature movie.

The group's producer, Erik Jacobsen, also produced Norman Greenbaum's 'Spirit In The Sky', and became Chris Isaak's producer. The Lovin' Spoonful's only known reunion was for their appearance in Paul Simon's 1980 movie, 'One Trick Pony', in which they were briefly seen performing 'Do You Believe In Magic?'.

MY GENERATION

THE WHO (1965)

SIDE ONE
Out In The Street (Townshend)
I Don't Mind (Brown)
The Good's Gone (Townshend)
La-La-La-Lies (Townshend)
Much Too Much (Pavey/Doonican)
My Generation (Townshend)

SIDE TWO
The Kids Are Alright (Townshend)
Please Please Please (Brown)
It's Not True (Townshend)
I'm A Man (McDaniel)
A Legal Matter (Townshend)
The Ox
(Townshend/Moon/Entwistle/Hopkins)

Produced by Shel Talmy
Total running time: 36.29

Released in the UK by Brunswick Records
and in the US by Decca Records

The Who proved themselves exciting innovators with *My Generation*. It also showed that in the great Pete Townshend this West London quartet had a songwriter fit to rank with the finest contemporary British talents.

Not that The Who were his backing band. Each member was special: Roger Daltrey was an aggressive and charismatic vocalist; Keith Moon, a quite unique drummer (whose self-destructive tendencies contributed to his death in 1978 at the age of 31); the reliable John Entwistle was on bass, content to leave the talking to his colleagues.

This album's most obvious instant highlight was its title track, still widely regarded as the group's anthem. Its oft-quoted line in which the protagonist hopes he dies before he gets old is one that Townshend must regret writing, as it has been thrown back at him ever since whenever he releases anything new.

Daltrey's spluttering fury as he asks: 'Why don't you all f-f-fade away?' couldn't fail to alienate the older people whose age he hoped never to reach, and at the same time strongly attracted young fans. A UK Top 3 hit, it was a surprisingly minor US chart item.

The inclusion of three respectable cover versions, two from James Brown and Bo Diddley's 'I'm A Man', was an interesting nod to prevailing trends.

Other notable tracks included the instrumental 'The Ox' and 'The Kids Are Alright', which was used as the title of the group's 1979 filmed career retrospective.

LEGAL MATTERS

The Who's early British releases were on Brunswick, but soon after this album emerged they signed with Robert Stigwood's Reaction label. Their first single under the new contract was 'Substitute', but with a dispute growing between the group's management and producer Talmy over the latter's continuing involvement, Brunswick swiftly responded by rush-releasing 'A Legal Matter' as a single. It charted, but outside the Top 30, whereas the newer track reached the Top 5.

Later in 1966, Reaction followed-up their hit with 'I'm A Boy', which was similarly jeopardised by Brunswick's release of 'The Kids Are Alright' as a 45, but with the same result – the new single made the Top 3, the album track stopped outside the Top 30. After a third single for Reaction, 'Happy Jack', the group left the label. It was a sizeable hit (promoted with a classic short film – pre-video – largely featuring the maniacal Moon) while their second album, A Quick One (While He's Away), was also released on Reaction. Its lengthy title track was described as 'Tommy's dad': it was Townshend's first attempt at writing something more expansive than a three-minute hit. The 10 minute story, featuring such characters as Ivor The Engine Driver, was in essence a rock opera, albeit a short one.

SOUNDS OF SILENCE

SIMON & GARFUNKEL (1966)

SIDE ONE
The Sounds Of Silence (Paul Simon)
Leaves That Are Green (Paul Simon)
Blessed (Paul Simon)
Kathy's Song (Paul Simon)
Somewhere They Can't Find Me (Paul Simon)
Anji (Davy Graham)

SIDE TWO
Homeward Bound (Paul Simon)
Richard Cory (Paul Simon)
A Most Peculiar Man (Paul Simon)
April Come She Will (Paul Simon)
We've Got A Groovy Thing Going
(Paul Simon)
I Am A Rock (Paul Simon)

Produced by Bob Johnston
Total running time: 31.56

Released in the US by Columbia Records and
in the UK by CBS Records

Sounds Of Silence was Simon & Garfunkel's second LP and included several songs which had previously appeared either on their 1964 debut *Wednesday Morning 3 A.M.* ('The Sounds Of Silence' and the title track, rewritten as 'Somewhere They Can't Find Me') or on Simon's 1965 solo album recorded in London, *The Paul Simon Songbook* ('I Am A Rock', 'Leaves That Are Green', 'April Come She Will', 'The Sounds Of Silence', 'A Most Peculiar Man' and 'Kathy's Song').

Wednesday Morning had been a flop until a radio disc jockey in Boston, Massachusetts, began playing 'Sounds Of Silence' from the LP. This excited enough interest for producer Tom Wilson, who had worked on the original acoustic recordings, to add an electric backing to the track (without Simon or

Garfunkel's knowledge) and it became a US Number 1 hit.

Simon at the time was living and working in Europe, while Garfunkel had given up music and was at university studying for a master's degree, but they were immediately rushed into the studio to make this second album, which included few new songs, although the reworkings of the songs from previous LPs improved on the originals.

Both 'Homeward Bound' (one of the new songs) and 'I Am A Rock' were US Top 10 hits and the duo's first two UK hits. The album itself peaked just outside the US Top 20 (but was subsequently certified triple platinum) and reached the UK Top 20. The opening couplet of 'Leaves That Are Green' was copied verbatim by UK singer/songwriter Billy Bragg in his song, 'A New England', a 1985 UK Top 10 hit for Kirsty MacColl.

ANIMATED CHARACTERS

After their shortlived fame as Tom & Jerry in 1958, Paul Simon (aka Jerry Landis) and Art Garfunkel (Tom Graph) drifted apart, attending different universities, although Simon attempted to remain involved in the music business by recording a number of singles under such names as True Taylor, Jerry Landis and, most successfully, Tico & The Triumphs (whose early 1962 single, 'Motorcycle', just crept into the US Top 100 for one week). Almost exactly a year later, in January 1963, 'The Lone Teen Ranger' (a Jerry Landis single) managed three weeks at the bottom of the US Top 100, but these minor successes were more than Garfunkel achieved with his singles released under the name of Artie Garr.

In 1964, Simon visited Europe, and became a familiar figure on the UK folk circuit, which is where he first heard 'Anji', the complex but brilliant guitar piece written by British folk performer Davy Graham. During this time, Simon recorded The Paul Simon Songbook in just over one hour at the London studios of CBS Records, and reputedly received an advance payment of £90 ($220).

IF YOU CAN BELIEVE YOUR EYES AND EARS

THE MAMAS & THE PAPAS (1966)

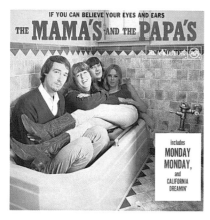

SIDE ONE
Monday Monday (Phillips)
Straight Shooter (Phillips)
Got A Feelin' (Doherty/Phillips)
I Call Your Name (Lennon/McCartney)
Do You Want To Dance (Freeman)
Go Where You Wanna Go (Phillips)

SIDE TWO
California Dreamin' (Phillips)
Spanish Harlem (Leiber/Spector)
Somebody Groovy (Phillips)
Hey Girl (J. & M. Phillips)
You Baby (Sloan/Barri)
The 'In' Crowd (Page)

Produced by Lou Adler
Total running time: 34.40

Released in the US on Dunhill Records and in the UK on RCA Records

The Mamas & The Papas, an archetypal '60s group, looked and performed like hippie royalty, which they were. A vocal quartet comprising two males (John Phillips, schooled at a military academy, and Denny Doherty, a Canadian) and two females (Michelle Gilliam, a beautiful model who had married Phillips, and the amply-proportioned Cass Elliott), the group evolved during a holiday in the Virgin Islands. Phillips, bored with New York, had convinced Michelle and Doherty to accompany him there in early 1965.

They were joined by Elliott, who had romantic aspirations on Doherty. The jaunt was financed by Phillips's American Express card, and with little money available for entertainment, the quartet lived on the beach, perfecting what would become their trademark stunning vocal harmonies.

Back in New York, John Phillips wrote 'California Dreamin'', and the quartet drove across the US to Los Angeles where Barry McGuire (whom Phillips knew from the folk circuit) introduced them to Dunhill Records, the label which had released his chart-topping 'Eve Of Destruction' hit in 1965.

Lou Adler, who had produced hits for Jan & Dean and Johnny Rivers, signed the group, immediately recognising their unique qualities. 'California Dreamin'', their debut single, sold a million copies. 'Monday Monday', released as a follow-up single, topped the US chart, again selling a million copies.

This debut album also reached Number 1 in the US chart and itself sold a million during its two-year residency.

SOLO INSTRUMENTALIST

As well as writing both the hit singles and five other songs here, John Phillips, the only member of the quartet who was also an instrumentalist, provided guitar backing, and was also responsible for all the group's vocal arrangements, which were written in sincere tribute to '50s vocal group The Four Freshmen. If he was the creative heart of the quartet, 'Mama' Cass was its best-loved member, but after she left the group for an intermittently successful solo career in 1968, the meteoric rise to fame of The Mamas & The Papas was balanced by an equally meteoric fall from grace, amid recriminations and lawsuits. During a career lasting a little over two years, they released five albums, four of which went gold.

In 1967, Phillips also composed the 'flower power' anthem, 'San Francisco (Wear Flowers In Your Hair)' for Scott McKenzie, another erstwhile member of The Journeymen, while the group were prominent members of the committee headed by Lou Adler which organised the pioneering Monterey Pop Festival in 1966.

'Mama' Cass died of a heart attack during a visit to London in 1974 at the age of only 32, and Phillips spent five years in jail during the '80s on drug charges.

SOLID GOLD SOUL

VARIOUS ARTISTS (1966)

Produced by: Buddy Killen (Joe Tex tracks); Steve Cropper (Otis Redding tracks); Jerry Leiber & Mike Stoller ('Stand By Me'); Ahmet Ertegun ('Don't Play That Song'); 'Jerry Wexler & Bert Berns ('Just Out Of Reach'); Jerry Wexler ('Got To Get You Off My Mind'); Steve Cropper & Jerry Wexler (Wilson Pickett tracks); Steve Cropper & Jim Stewart ('See-Saw'); Don Covay & Horace Ott ('Mercy, Mercy')
Total running time: 32.07
Released in the US and the UK by Atlantic Records

The mid-'60s saw a strong surge of popularity for soul/R&B music, with its twin spearheads of Motown (from Detroit) and Atlantic (from New York).

This LP introduced many British record buyers not only to soul stars signed to Atlantic itself (King, Burke, Covay and Pickett), but also to two major names signed to labels connected with Atlantic – Otis Redding (from Stax/Volt Records in Memphis) and Joe Tex (from Dial Records in Nashville).

British youth found this collection the perfect introduction to some of the emergent acts who were being praised by The Beatles and The Stones.

It was less significant in the US, where the tracks were already well known, mostly as Top 30 hits in the pop chart. Half the tracks involved guitarist Steve Cropper (of Booker T. & the MGs, the Stax Records house band) as writer and/or producer, and the various producers include some of the most legendary names of the era – including Atlantic President Ertegun, who reversed his name for the credit on 'Don't Play That Song', Leiber & Stoller (aka Elmo Glick) and Wexler and Berns.

SIDE ONE
Got To Get You Off My Mind (Burke) (1)
Don't Fight It (Pickett/Cropper) (2)
I Want To (Do Everything For You) (Tex) (3)
See-Saw (Covay/Cropper) (4)
Don't Play That Song (Nugetre) (5)
Mr. Pitiful (Redding/Cropper) (6)

SIDE TWO
In The Midnight Hour (Pickett/Cropper) (2)
Hold What You've Got (Tex) (3)
Mercy, Mercy (Covay/Ott) (4)
I've Been Loving You Too Long (Redding) (6)
Just Out Of Reach (Stewart) (1)
Stand By Me (King/Glick) (5)

THE ARTISTS
(1) Solomon Burke, (2) Wilson Pickett,
(3) Joe Tex, (4) Don Covay, (5) Ben E. King,
(6) Otis Redding

GOLDEN GREATS

Two of the artists whose work appeared on Solid Gold Soul are deceased. Otis Redding was killed in a plane crash in late 1967, aged 26, and Joe Tex died of a heart attack in 1982, aged 49.

Tex (Joseph Arrington Jr.), was, appropriately, from Texas. He was noted for his gospel-influenced 'testifying' approach, exemplified by 'Hold What You've Got', his first US Top 10 hit. Nashville entrepreneur Buddy Killen launched Dial Records specifically to release tracks by Tex.

As a teenager, Solomon Burke broadcast as the 'Wonder Boy Preacher' from Solomon's Temple, a church his grandmother founded for him. The Rolling Stones covered Burke's 'Everybody Needs Somebody To Love' in 1965.

Wilson Pickett, from Prattsville, Alabama, released 38 US pop hits between 1963 and 1973. Don Covay, from South Carolina, was the least prominent of the artists on this album, and was rarely heard of after the early '70s.

Ben E. King first emerged in 1960 as lead vocalist of The Drifters on their first US Number 1, 'Save The Last Dance For Me', and is the most visible of the surviving artists on the album, due to the chart-topping revival of 'Stand By Me' in 1986.

AFTERMATH

THE ROLLING STONES (1966)

SIDE ONE
Mother's Little Helper (Jagger/Richard)
Stupid Girl (Jagger/Richard)
Lady Jane (Jagger/Richard)
Under My Thumb (Jagger/Richard)
Doncha Bother Me (Jagger/Richard)
Goin' Home (Jagger/Richard)

SIDE TWO
Flight 505 (Jagger/Richard)
High And Dry (Jagger/Richard)
Out Of Time (Jagger/Richard)
It's Not Easy (Jagger/Richard)
I Am Waiting (Jagger/Richard)
Take It Or Leave It (Jagger/Richard)
Think (Jagger/Richard)
What To Do (Jagger, Richard)

Produced by Andrew Loog Oldham
Total running time: 52.23
Released in the UK by Decca Records and in the US by London Records

The US version omitted 'Mother's Little Helper', 'Out Of Time', 'Take It Or Leave It' and 'What To Do' and included 'Paint It Black'.

Aftermath is the most fully realised Rolling Stones album. It was also the first on which the songs were all Jagger/Richard originals. Their songwriting had matured considerably, as they created the songs on this LP that were hits for the group themselves and for other acts.

'Mother's Little Helper' was a US Top 10 for The Stones; 'Lady Jane' made the US Top 30 for The Stones and the UK Top 30 for David Garrick; 'Under My Thumb' was a UK Top 50 hit for The Who; 'Out Of Time' was a UK Number 1 for Chris Farlowe; 'Take It Or Leave It' made the UK Top 40 for The Searchers; and 'Think' was a UK Top 40 hit for Chris Farlowe.

Few albums by The Beatles had spawned so many hit singles, and never again would their greatest rivals prove so influential as songwriters.

Aftermath was recorded at RCA Studios in Hollywood with engineer Dave Hassinger, who had worked on their previous album, *Out Of Our Heads*. Arranger Jack Nitzsche (a Phil Spector associate) shared keyboard duties with the faithful Ian Stewart.

The album has been cited as illustrating Mick Jagger's love/hate relationship with women, from the contempt of 'Mother's Little Helper' for those who take drugs to give them energy (pots and kettles?) to the highly dismissive 'Stupid Girl' and 'Under My Thumb' and the ultimate put-down of 'Out Of Time'. But another side of the group was exemplified on the 11-minute-plus 'Goin' Home', on which they gloriously rock out in spectacular style.

A MASTERPIECE BY ANY NAME

Initially, Aftermath was titled Could You Walk On Water?, *but Decca Records, with whom the group maintained an uneasy relationship, made it clear that they could not possibly release it unless the title was changed. On this occasion, the group complied. They would get their revenge in 1970 when they completed their contractual obligations to Decca Records by delivering one final unreleased track titled 'Cocksucker Blues', which has never been legally released for obvious reasons, but has been widely bootlegged.*

Aftermath topped the UK chart for eight weeks (and reached the US Top 3), but its most familiar track, 'Out Of Time', was donated to London R&B vocalist Chris Farlowe, whose version, produced by Mick Jagger, was released on Immediate Records, the label launched by Andrew Loog Oldham, the group's producer and manager. The Stones eventually had a minor single hit with a slightly different recording of the song when it was released by Decca in 1975.

PET SOUNDS

THE BEACH BOYS (1966)

Produced by Brian Wilson
Total running time: 37.01
Released in the US & the UK by Capitol Records

SIDE ONE
Wouldn't It Be Nice (B. Wilson/T. Asher)
You Still Believe In Me (B. Wilson/T. Asher)
That's Not Me (B. Wilson/T. Asher)
Don't Talk (Put Your Head On My Shoulder)
(B. Wilson/T. Asher)
I'm Waiting For The Day (B. Wilson/M. Love)
Let's Go Away For Awhile (Brian Wilson)
Sloop John B (Arr. Brian Wilson)

SIDE TWO
God Only Knows (B. Wilson/T. Asher)
I Know There's An Answer
(B. Wilson/T. Sachen)
Here Today (B. Wilson/T. Asher)
I Just Wasn't Made For These Times
(B. Wilson/T. Asher)
Pet Sounds (Brian Wilson)
Caroline No (B. Wilson/T. Asher)

The finest Beach Boys album, *Pet Sounds* was inspired by Brian Wilson, who had stopped playing live with the group in late 1964. His place had been taken first by Glen Campbell (later a famous country singer) and then by Bruce Johnston, from Los Angeles group The Rip Chords.

Wilson still wrote all the group's songs and produced their records, and he regarded *Rubber Soul* by The Beatles as a challenge. He was determined to equal or better it with his own masterpiece. Creating backing tracks with a live orchestra, he sang lead on most of the album .

The group were on tour without him when he conceived *Pet Sounds*, so Brian required a songwriting partner to replace Mike Love, with whom he had written many of the Beach Boys' previous songs. For this album he worked mostly with lyricist Tony Asher.

The album was preceded by a US & UK Top 3 single, 'Sloop John B' (a song familiar to UK audiences as skiffle king Lonnie Donegan's 1960 version under the title 'I Wanna Go Home' had been a Top 5 hit).

The next US single coupled 'Wouldn't It Be Nice' and 'God Only Knows' – in the US, the former track made the Top 10, the latter the Top 40, but in the UK 'God Only Knows' was a Top 3 hit. Before 'Sloop John B' emerged, 'Caroline No' had been released as a Brian Wilson solo 45, reaching the US Top 40, but flopping in the UK.

A MODERN EPIC

If Pet Sounds was undoubtedly Brian Wilson's finest artistic achievement in terms of sustained excellence, his group's next 45, 'Good Vibrations', was arguably superior to any other track Wilson will ever create. This universally acclaimed epic topped the singles charts on both sides of the Atlantic, selling several million copies. Recorded in four studios over a period of six months, it was intended as one of the tracks on the group's follow-up album to Pet Sounds, which was to be titled Smile. However, this was an even more complex project than Pet Sounds, and Brian used drugs in an attempt to progress with the album.

During the recording of 'Fire', part of 'The Elements', the studio in which he was working, was damaged by a fire, for which Brian thought he was responsible, whereupon he locked the tapes in a vault. The album was never legally released, although certain tracks from it emerged.

Brian Wilson grew increasingly eccentric at this time, installing a grand piano in a large box of sand, theoretically to feel the sand on his feet (recreating happy childhood feelings), but in reality to provide toilet facilities for his dogs. He also stayed in bed for months, and his lack of exercise resulted in his becoming obese.

BLONDE ON BLONDE

BOB DYLAN (1966)

SIDE ONE
Rainy Day Women Nos.12 & 35 (B. Dylan)
Pledging My Time (B. Dylan)
Visions Of Johanna (B. Dylan)
One Of Us Must Know (Sooner Or Later)
(B. Dylan)

SIDE TWO
I Want You (B. Dylan)
Stuck Inside Of Mobile With Thee
(B. Dylan)
Leopard-Skin Pill-Box Hat (B. Dylan)
Just Like A Woman (B. Dylan)

SIDE THREE
Most Likely You Go Your Way
And I'll Go Mine (B. Dylan)
Temporary Like Achilles (B. Dylan)
Absolutely Sweet Marie (B. Dylan)
4th Time Around (B. Dylan)
Obviously 5 Believers (B. Dylan)

SIDE FOUR
Sad Eyed Lady Of The Lowlands (B. Dylan)

Produced by Bob Johnston
Total running time: 72.16
Released in the US by Columbia Records and
in the UK by CBS Records

Blonde On Blonde was voted the second best album of all time in 1977 by an international panel of rock critics (after *Sergeant Pepper*) and third best in an equivalent 1987 poll (after *Pepper* and Bruce Springsteen's second album *The Wild, The Innocent and The E. Street Shuffle*). *Blonde On Blonde* remains Bob Dylan's masterpiece.

It is the centrepiece of his best three albums (early '60s Dylan is best-represented by *The Times They Are A-Changin'*, the later, mature years by *Blood On The Tracks*), with over an hour of poetically verbose lyrics often delivered in a nasal drawl over a hotshot session band of Nashville's finest.

Three of those musicians would later go on to form the backbone of Area Code 615, the group of session players who made two critically-acclaimed albums in 1969 and 1970.

Bass player Wayne Moss and drummer Kenny Buttrey played on zillions of other records during this era, and harmonica virtuoso Charlie McCoy worked on even more.

It's something of a minor shame that McCoy didn't provide Dylan with a few tips on constructive harp playing, to judge by the latter's tune-shy squalling on the track 'Absolutely Sweet Marie' played above a backing that is as tight as a straitjacket.

Moss also played guitar on 'I Want You', and a Dylan expert suggests that McCoy simultaneously plays electric bass with his left hand and trumpet with his right on 'Most Likely You Go Your Way And I'll Go Mine'.

Al Kooper, who had played organ so effectively on *Highway 61 Revisited*'s 'Like A Rolling Stone', was one of two non-Nashville pickers who were credited on the album, the other being guitarist Jaime 'Robbie' Robertson, who was the only representative of The Band, the mainly Canadian combo who were Dylan's regular backing group during this period.

However, the same Dylan expert also suggests that Robertson's colleague, bass player Rick Danko, is on 'One Of Us Must Know' (a UK Top 40 single), which was recorded in New York in

January 1966, the month before the Nashville sessions which produced the rest of the tracks.

The rowdy opening track 'Rainy Day Women''s party-like atmosphere and hook line about everybody getting stoned made it a great favourite among those who enjoyed illegal stimulation.

It was also the biggest of several hit singles included on the album, making the US & UK Top 10. The contrastingly gentle 'I Want You' reached the UK & US Top 20.

'Just Like A Woman' was a US Top 40 hit for Dylan and a UK Top 40 hit for Manfred Mann, the latter's first featuring new vocalist Mike d'Abo.

The biting 'Leopard-Skin Pill-Box Hat' was a minor US hit single – the song's storyline about Dylan's distaste for a bimbo wearing such a fashion accessory and its ironic query about the feelings of the skin's original owner doubtless seemed rather too serious for many singles buyers.

But the epic work here was 'Sad Eyed Lady Of The Lowlands', more than 11 minutes of sublime poetry in the form of a heartfelt love song to Dylan's new wife, Sara, which provoked innumerable lonely hearts advertisements from people who wanted to be as deeply in love as Dylan obviously was.

Despite that, they probably had no more idea than anyone else about the meaning of the line that refers to his partner's warehouse eyes and the Arabian drums.

It's interesting to note that the original track listing on the LP featured the 'Stuck Inside Of Mobile' title as it is listed here, but later issues retitled the song 'Stuck Inside Of Mobile With The Memphis Blues Again'.

THE CRASH

Less than three months after Blonde On Blonde *had been released, Bob Dylan was involved in a serious accident while riding his Triumph motorcycle near Woodstock in New York state.*

He spent some time in hospital with concussion and broken vertebrae in his neck, and he was forced to remain in bed for around a month, in stark contrast to his frenetic activity of the previous year, when he had seemed to be on an almost endless tour.

Some suggested either that the crash had been fabricated to allow Dylan to escape from the treadmill of constant touring and recording, or that the accident occurred because of his frantic lifestyle.

Whatever the cause, Dylan was effectively silent for the first half of 1967, although a compilation Greatest Hits *album was released on both sides of the Atlantic early in the year. It wasn't until October that Dylan officially returned to the studio to resume his recording career.*

However, it later became clear that Dylan had been working with The Band at their Woodstock house named Big Pink, which later inspired the title of the group's debut album, Music From Big Pink.

BLUES BREAKERS

JOHN MAYALL WITH ERIC CLAPTON (1966)

SIDE ONE
All Your Love (Rush)
Hideaway (King/Thompson)
Little Girl (Mayall)
Another Man (Arranged Mayall)
Double Crossin' Time (Mayall/Clapton)
What'd I Say (Charles)

SIDE TWO
Key To Love (Mayall)
Parchman Farm (Allison)
Have You Heard (Mayall)
Ramblin' On My Mind (Johnson)
Steppin' Out (L. C. Frazier)
It Ain't Right (Jacobs)

Produced by Mike Vernon
Total running time: 36.51

Released in the UK by Decca Records and in the US by London Records

Guitarist Eric 'Slowhand' Clapton had left The Yardbirds in March 1965, and was instantly invited by John Mayall (vocals, keyboards, harmonica) to join his group, The Bluesbreakers, which also included John McVie (bass) and Hughie Flint (drums).

Clapton's presence was a considerable boost for the band, which quickly became one of the most popular acts on the British circuit. However, Clapton's 15 months with Mayall's Bluesbreakers involved several personnel changes – Clapton himself went AWOL in the summer of 1965 for three months on a trip to Greece. He was replaced by temporary guitarists, the last of whom, Peter Green, was with Mayall for less than a week before Clapton returned.

During Clapton's absence, McVie had been fired for drinking too much and

replaced by Jack Bruce from the Graham Bond Organisation, but Bruce left after a month for financial reasons, and McVie was invited back. At this point, with the band's line-up exactly as it had been when Clapton first arrived, producer Mike Vernon convinced Decca that he should record an album by this quartet. Mayall allowed Clapton to display his influences, recording songs by Otis Rush, Freddie King and Robert Johnson, whose 'Ramblin' On My Mind' has the distinction of being the first track recorded with a lead vocal by Clapton.

'Double Crossing Time' was Mayall's reaction to the sudden departure of Jack Bruce to the Manfred Mann group, and 'Steppin' Out' had been recorded by Clapton a few weeks before as leader of Eric Clapton & The Powerhouse, a studio group formed to contribute to a compilation album, *What's Shakin'*.

FATHER FIGURE OF BRITISH BLUES

If Alexis Korner could claim to be the Godfather of British R&B by dint of his discovery of most of The Rolling Stones, one of those encouraged by Korner, John Mayall, could make a similar claim. Apart from Clapton, other members of The Bluesbreakers at various times during the '60s included Peter Green, first Clapton's temporary stand-in when the latter went to Greece, and later a permanent replacement when the band also included John McVie and drummer Mick Fleetwood, who founded Fleetwood Mac with Green in 1967.

Green's replacement was Mick Taylor from The Gods. Taylor left The Bluesbreakers in 1969 to join The Rolling Stones. Hughie Flint, the drummer on this album, moved on to McGuinness-Flint, and then to The Blues Band.

Bluesbreakers who were already celebrated before joining Mayall included Canned Heat members Harvey Mandel (guitar) and Larry Taylor (bass), US violin star 'Sugarcane' Harris, and Duster Bennett, a one-man band who made three solo albums between 1968 and 1970 before his stint with Mayall.

REVOLVER

THE BEATLES (1966)

Produced by George Martin
Total running time: 35.01
Released in the UK by Parlophone Records
and in the US by Capitol Records

SIDE ONE
Taxman (Harrison)
Eleanor Rigby (Lennon/McCartney)
I'm Only Sleeping (Lennon/McCartney)
Love You To (Harrison)
Here, There And Everywhere
(Lennon/McCartney)
Yellow Submarine (Lennon/McCartney)
She Said, She Said (Lennon/McCartney)

SIDE TWO
Good Day Sunshine (Lennon/McCartney)
And Your Bird Can Sing (Lennon/McCartney)
For No One (Lennon/McCartney)
Doctor Robert (Lennon/McCartney)
I Want To Tell You (Harrison)
Got To Get You Into My Life
(Lennon/McCartney)
Tomorrow Never Knows
(Lennon/McCartney)

As usual, the US version of the latest Beatles LP was slightly different, omitting 'And Your Bird Can Sing', 'I'm Only Sleeping' and 'Doctor Robert', all of which had been included on Yesterday & Today, a US-only Beatles LP released two months before Revolver.

'Eleanor Rigby', the sad tale of a lonely woman, and which featured an eight-piece string section, has been the subject of innumerable cover versions over the years, including versions by Ray Charles and Aretha Franklin.

Paul McCartney was originally inspired to write the song when the implied rhythm in the name Daisy Hawkins, which he saw over a shop in Bristol, appealed to him, and after minor changes became Eleanor Rigby.

'Love You To' featured George Harrison on a sitar, with tabla (hand drum) played by Anil Bhagwat, an Indian musician, and 'Doctor Robert' was a real person in New York who would acquire drugs for needy pop stars if he was asked.

'Tomorrow Never Knows' features John Lennon's vocal fed through a Leslie speaker (more often used with the Hammond organ), as Lennon wanted his voice to sound as though it were coming from a Tibetan hill-top !

The award-winning album sleeve was designed by Klaus Voorman, a German who had befriended The Beatles when they were playing in the clubs of Hamburg during the early '60s.

MARKET FORCES

Revolver *was the seventh album by The Beatles to be released in the UK, yet it was the group's 16th LP in the US. Only a handful of tracks which did not appear on UK albums were included on US LPs, including a few tracks from UK singles and EPs, plus German language versions of 'She Loves You' ('Sie Liebt Dich') and 'I Want To Hold Your Hand' ('Komm, Gib Mir Deine Hand'). This gives some indication of the differing marketing practices on opposite sides of the Atlantic.*

Thus US albums such as Something New, Beatles '65, Beatles VI *and* Yesterday And Today *mainly comprised tracks which had been omitted from US versions of original UK albums, often due to the US custom of limiting the number of tracks on an album for reasons relating to music publishing copyright fees, although such restrictions did not apply in the UK.*

Yesterday And Today *caused enormous controversy when it was originally released in the US, as its sleeve showed the group in butcher's aprons surrounded by chunks of meat and mutilated dolls, which many felt was an inappropriate image for the biggest group in the world.*

The album was swiftly withdrawn and reissued with a more orthodox sleeve photograph.

RIVER DEEP - MOUNTAIN HIGH

IKE & TINA TURNER (1966)

Produced by Phil Spector * and Ike Turner **
Total running time: 32.42
Released in the UK by London Records and
in the US by Philles Records
The first US release of the album (in 1969) included 'I'll Never Need More Than This'
(Spector/Barry/Greenwich) which was produced by Phil Spector. It excluded 'You're So Fine'

SIDE ONE

River Deep - Mountain High
(Spector/Greenwich/Barry) *
I Idolize You (I. Turner)**
A Love Like Yours (Don't Come Knocking
Every Day) (E. & B. Holland/Dozier) *
A Fool In Love (I. Turner) **
Make 'Em Wait (I. Turner) **
Hold On Baby (Greenwich/Barry) *

SIDE TWO

Save The Last Dance For Me
(Pomus/Shuman) *
Oh Baby (Things Ain't What
They Used To Be) (Harris) **
Everyday I Have To Cry (Alexander) *
Such A Fool For You (Turner) **
It's Gonna Work Out Fine (Senaca/Lee) **
You're So Fine (Finney/Schofield/West) **

Ike & Tina Turner's early '60s hits like 'A Fool In Love', 'I Idolize You' and 'It's Gonna Work Out Fine' were all included on this dynamic album. It also included the Phil Spector-produced single 'River Deep – Mountain High', a masterpiece bordering on genius. As a US 45, it was a flop, although in the UK it was a Top 3 hit. Its failure in the US forced Spector to become a virtual recluse and, for that reason, this album was not released in the US until 1969.

The Turners had first met Phil Spector when they were booked along with acts like The Byrds, The Lovin' Spoonful and The Ronettes to appear in 'The Big TNT Show', a 1965 live concert film for which Spector was musical director.

It had been 18 months since Spector's last huge hit ('You've Lost That Lovin' Feelin'' by The Righteous Brothers), and the reaction of the predominantly white audience to their wild stage act alerted Spector to Tina's potential as an act he could profitably produce.

He was, however, wary of Ike's reputation as a violent individual who was known to carry a gun with which he could enforce his decisions both on the road and in the studio.

Spector, who was dwarfed by Ike physically, was only interested in Tina's soulful voice, and convinced Ike to stay away from the studio by promising him future work.

ROCKET MAN

Ike Turner was born in 1931, and was a child prodigy who backed such noted bluesmen as Sonny Boy Williamson II and Robert Nighthawk while still in his early teens.

After working as a disc jockey, he formed his own group, The Kings Of Rhythm, who were the backing band on 'Rocket 88', a 1951 single on the Sun label by Jackie Brenston, which experts have called the very first rock'n'roll track. Becoming a session musician, Turner recorded with Howlin' Wolf, B.B. King and others, before in 1956 meeting an 18-year-old girl named Anna Mae Bullock, whom he married two years later. By then she had changed her name to Tina Turner and was the lead vocalist of the Ike & Tina Turner Revue.

Their first hit single, 'A Fool In Love', came in 1960, and was the first of five US Top 10 R&B hits by mid-1962.

With a trio of female backing singers, The Ikettes, the Revue became a major attraction, largely due to Tina's highly energetic dancing and her sexy vocal style, although their success had somewhat declined, largely due to Ike's increasing drug and alcohol abuse, by the time they met Phil Spector.

THE MONKEES

THE MONKEES (1966)

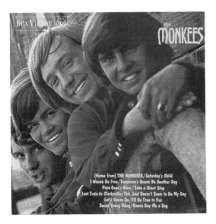

SIDE ONE
Theme From 'The Monkees' (Boyce/Hart) *
Saturday's Child (Gates) *
I Wanna Be Free (Boyce/Hart) **
Tomorrow's Gonna Be Another Day
(Boyce/Venet) **
Papa Gene's Blues (Nesmith) ***
Take A Giant Step (Goffin/King) **

SIDE TWO
Last Train To Clarksville (Boyce/Hart) **
This Just Doesn't Seem To Be My Day
(Boyce/Hart) *
Let's Dance On (Boyce/Hart) *
I'll Be True To You (Goffin/Titleman) *
Sweet Young Thing (Nesmith/Goffin/King) ***
Gonna Buy Me A Dog (Boyce/Hart) **

Produced by Tommy Boyce, Bobby Hart &
Jack Keller *****,
Tommy Boyce & Bobby Hart ******,
Michael Nesmith *******

Total running time: 29.43
Released in the US on Colgems Records and
in the UK on RCA Records

The Monkees, a quartet of young men in their early twenties, were hired after auditions involving 400 people to play the part of a wacky Beatlesque group in a US TV series that became hugely popular.

Musicians Michael Nesmith and Peter Tork were joined by two ex-child actors, Mickey Dolenz, an American who had starred as TV's 'Circus Boy', and Davy Jones, from Manchester in England, who had played the title role in the London production of the musical, 'Oliver'.

When the TV shows were an immediate hit, the group started releasing records, opening their US chart account with a Number 1 single, 'Last Train To Clarksville', and this album, which also topped the chart.

A second single, 'I'm A Believer', zoomed to Number 1 in the US in early 1967, and was also a Number 1 hit in the UK, where it belatedly brought 'Clarksville' into the Top 30.

This dragged the Monkees' first album into the UK chart, which it topped for seven weeks. The man behind this overnight success, the size and speed of which few could have predicted, was a New Yorker, Don Kirshner, who had established an enviable reputation as a successful music publisher.

Among the writers he discovered were Tommy Boyce & Bobby Hart. Their compositions dominated this debut album. More than 50% of the songs were credited to them, including both the 'Clarksville' hit and the theme song of the TV series.

MONKEE BUSINESS

The main problem experienced by The Monkees during their brief career was that Kirshner would not initially allow them to play on their records (although Dolenz was the lead vocalist on much of this album, with occasional assistance from Jones). Instrumental backing was largely provided by session musicians.

Texan Michael Nesmith, whose trademark in the TV show was a woolly hat, insisted on the inclusion of two of his own compositions, one co-written with Goffin & King, on which he and Tork took an active part in the recording studio, but Kirshner clearly (and incorrectly) regarded these departures from his formula as necessary irritants. He was unwilling to believe that members of the group could have the ability to write a song suitable for release as a single. However, he may have had reason to doubt his beliefs when one of Nesmith's compositions, 'Mary, Mary', from the group's second album, More Of The Monkees, was recorded by Paul Butterfield's Blues Band on their second album East West, gaining The Monkees some much-needed credibility among their peers.

ROY ORBISON SINGS DON GIBSON

ROY ORBISON (1966)

Produced by Wesley Rose & Jim Vienneau
Total running time: 29.29

SIDE ONE
(I'd Be) A Legend In My Time (Gibson)
(Yes) I'm Hurting (Gibson)
The Same Street (Gibson)
Far Far Away (Gibson)
Big Hearted Me (Gibson)
Sweet Dreams (Gibson)

SIDE TWO
Oh, Such A Stranger (Gibson)
Blue, Blue Day (Gibson)
What About Me (Gibson)
Give Myself A Party (Gibson)
Too Soon To Know (Gibson)
Lonesome Number One (Gibson)

Released in the US by MGM Records and in the UK by London Records

In early 1965, Roy Orbison had separated from his wife, Claudette (the subject of one of his best early compositions, which was a big hit for The Everly Brothers). He had also just moved from Monument Records, the label on which he had become a huge star, to MGM.

MGM had paid him an advance of a million dollars. It was not just the money that attracted Orbison and his manager, Wesley Rose, but the chance that MGM's parent film company would consider him for movie roles.

In mid-1966, Claudette died in a motorcycle accident, which not surprisingly produced a writer's block in her husband, especially as they had planned to re-marry.

However, MGM wanted some return on their million dollar investment, and strongly supported Wesley Rose's plan for Orbison to record an album's worth of songs by country singer/songwriter Don Gibson.

Gibson's songs were administered – another surprise – by Acuff-Rose, the music publishing company founded by Rose's father. Even so, the idea was good: Gibson, like Orbison, often wrote from the point of view of a victim of love.

Many of the songs featured on this album had been among Gibson's biggest hits, including 'Sweet Dreams' (a hit for Patsy Cline), 'Blue, Blue Day' (a 1958 US country Number 1 by Gibson himself) and other US country Top 10 hits such as 'Give Myself A Party' (1958), 'Lonesome Number One' (1961) and '(Yes) I'm Hurting' (1966).

Orbison was able to use the recording sessions as therapy, and 'Too Soon To Know' became his final US Top 3 single of the decade.

Roy Orbison is better-known for his string of hits during the early '60s, but this collection proved that he could interpret another artist's songs.

LASTING TALENT

Brought up in the West Texas town of Wink, Roy Orbison won a talent contest as a member of a hillbilly group, The Wink Westerners, and during the '50s his recordings were produced by both Norman Petty (who discovered Buddy Holly), and by Sam Phillips at Sun Records, where his first hit was 'Ooby Dooby'.

His early rockabilly-styled records were rarely successful, and in 1960, his second single for the newly launched Monument label, 'Only The Lonely', which he had written with Elvis Presley in mind and had also offered to The Everly Brothers, sold a million copies in reaching the US Top 3 and topping the UK chart.

It was followed in 1961/2 by three more million sellers, and he toured the UK regularly during the first half of the '60s, becoming one of the very few US stars to survive the 'British Beat' era, when the charts on both sides of the Atlantic were dominated by The Beatles, The Rolling Stones, and many other British acts.

BIG HITS (HIGH TIDE AND GREEN GRASS)

THE ROLLING STONES (1966)

SIDE ONE
**Have You Seen Your Mother, Baby, Standing
In The Shadows (Jagger/Richard)
Paint It Black (Jagger/Richard)
It's All Over Now (B. & S. Womack)
The Last Time (Jagger/Richard)
Heart Of Stone (Jagger/Richard)
Not Fade Away (Petty/Hardin)
Come On (Berry)**

SIDE TWO
**(I Can't Get No) Satisfaction
(Jagger/Richard)
Get Off Of My Cloud (Jagger/Richard)
As Tears Go By (Jagger/Richard/Oldham)
19th Nervous Breakdown (Jagger/Richard)
Lady Jane (Jagger/Richard)
Time Is On My Side (Meade/Norman)
Little Red Rooster (Dixon)**

Produced by Andrew Loog Oldham
Total running time: 39.55
*Released in the UK by Decca Records and in
the US by London Records*

The best 'Greatest Hits' compilation of the era and the quintessential Stones album, capturing the group at its very best.

The UK version of this album includes ten of the group's 11 hits up until that point, omitting 'I Wanna Be Your Man'.

The album includes six still familiar UK Number 1 hits: 'It's All Over Now', 'Little Red Rooster', 'The Last Time', 'Satisfaction', 'Get Off Of My Cloud' and 'Paint It Black'.

The US version, released a few months before the UK equivalent, omitted 'Have You Seen Your Mother', 'Paint It Black', 'Come On', 'Lady Jane' and 'Little Red Rooster', but included 'Tell Me (You're Coming Back)' (Jagger/Richard), 'Good Times, Bad Times' (Jagger/Richard) and 'Play With Fire' (Nanker/Phelge).

The album documents the move away from the group's classic cover versions towards the instant brilliance of the early Jagger & Richard originals.

The covers were Chuck Berry's 'Come On'; 'Not Fade Away' (originally the B-side of 'Oh Boy!', by Buddy Holly's group, The Crickets); 'It's All Over Now' (a minor US R&B hit by The Valentinos); 'Little Red Rooster' (a 1963 US Top 20 hit for Sam Cooke); and 'Time Is On My Side' (their first US Top 10 single).

At this point, The Stones were under the control of Andrew Loog Oldham, their first manager and producer, and the man who helped create their image as the bad boys of '60s rock.

POLITICAL MOVES

The group's internal politics at this time were relatively straightforward – Mick Jagger, Keith Richard and Brian Jones were the exotic stars, while the rhythm section of Bill Wyman and Charlie Watts were just that, the rhythm section.

Jones regarded The Rollin' Stones (as they were known initially) as his band, and was known as the band member who dared to experiment – the one who played sitar on 'Paint It Black', and the one who could seemingly coax a tune out of any stringed instrument.

Change arrived when Andrew Oldham became the group's manager and befriended Jagger and Richard, whereas Jones, the group's first sex symbol, swiftly became unreliable, partly due to his poor health (he suffered from asthma) and partly because of his prodigious drug intake. Jones was not a songwriter, and when Oldham urged Jagger and Richard to write original material for the group, Jones became further distanced from his erstwhile best friends, and sought solace in more and more artificial stimulation.

As he was eased out of the group that had been his idea in the first place, Jones felt increasingly isolated and he fell into a downward spiral from which he never recovered.

GREATEST HITS

THE TEMPTATIONS (1966)

Produced by Smokey Robinson *,
Norman Whitfield **,
Smokey Robinson & Ronald White ***

SIDE ONE
*The Way You Do The Things You Do
(Robinson/Rogers) *
My Girl (Robinson/White) ***
Ain't Too Proud To Beg (Holland/Whitfield) **
Don't Look Back (Robinson/White) ***
Get Ready (Robinson) *
Beauty Is Only Skin Deep (Whitfield/Holland) ***

SIDE TWO
*Since I Lost My Baby (Robinson/Moore) *
The Girl's Alright With Me (Holland/Whitfield) **
My Baby (Moore/Robinson/Rogers) ***
It's Growing (Robinson/Moore) *
I'll Be In Trouble (Robinson) *
Girl (Why You Wanna Make Me Blue)
(Holland/Whitfield) ***

Total running time: 34.07
Released on Gordy Records in the US
and Tamla Motown Records in the UK

Featuring the early classic line-up of this still-active R&B vocal quintet who were among Motown's biggest stars, the tracks here include their first 11 US hits, seven of which were written and produced by Smokey Robinson.

That initial Smokey-fuelled success ended when a suitable successor was discovered in Norman Whitfield, who piloted the group to even greater success with 'psychedelic soul', culminating in 1972's unforgettable single 'Papa Was A Rollin' Stone'.

Famed at this time almost as much for their superbly choreographed stage show as for their regular hits, the group's best-loved tracks here include 'My Girl' (their first US Number 1, which was also memorably covered by Otis Redding), 'Ain't Too Proud To Beg', a dramatic dance-floor favourite which was their first

UK Top 30 hit, the equally urgent 'Get Ready' and their debut US pop hit, 'The Way You Do The Things You Do'. It includes a fine example of Smokey's lyrical ingenuity: 'You've got a smile so bright, you know you could have been a candle, I'm holding you so tight, you know you should have been a handle'.

After an isolated early success with 'Girl (Why You Wanna Make Me Blue)', Norman Whitfield took over Robinson's writer/producer role, and followed 'Ain't Too Proud To Beg' with the equally memorable 'Beauty Is Only Skin Deep'.

Whitfield also provided the vast majority of the group's latterday hits, most of which he co-wrote with Barrett Strong, an early Motown star, whose first hit as an artist, 'Money (That's What I Want)', was covered by both The Beatles and The Rolling Stones.

LEAVING TEMPTATIONS BEHIND

By late 1971, only archetypal bass singer Melvin Franklin and Otis Williams remained of the quintet featured here, as erstwhile lead vocalists David Ruffin (in 1969) and Eddie Kendricks (with Paul Williams, in 1971), jumped ship for sporadic solo chart success which occurred soon after their departure, but which lasted a relatively short time. In 1985, Kendricks and Ruffin appeared onstage at Harlem's celebrated Apollo Theater with Daryl Hall & John Oates, who had made no secret of the inspiration provided by The Temptations in their formative years.

In 1968/9, Diana Ross & The Supremes recorded four US hit albums of 'duets' with The Temptations, the second of which, 1969's TCB (taking care of business) topped the US album chart. The Temptations were inducted into the Rock'n'Roll Hall Of Fame in 1989, Ruffin died of a drug overdose in 1991 and Kendricks of lung cancer in 1992.

DA CAPO

LOVE (1967)

SIDE ONE
Stephanie Knows Who (Arthur Lee)
Orange Skies (Bryan Maclean)
!Que Vida! (Arthur Lee)
Seven & Seven Is (Arthur Lee)
The Castle (Arthur Lee)
She Comes In Colors (Arthur Lee)

SIDE TWO
Revelation (Lee/Maclean/Echols/Forssi)

Produced by Paul A. Rothschild
Total running time: 36.18
Released in the US and UK on Elektra Records

The second Love album was instantly remarkable for the over-ambitious 'Revelation' (nearly 19 minutes and the complete Side Two). But the six songs on Side One easily compensated for its shortcomings: the urgent 'Stephanie' ; Maclean's soft ballad; the Latin-styled '!Que Vida!'; the frantic 'Seven And Seven Is' (their only US Top 40 hit); the acoustic guitar-dominated 'The Castle'; and the drugs and sex-influenced ballad, 'She Comes In Colors'.

Lyrically enigmatic, Love was fronted by the charismatic Memphis-born Arthur Lee as lead singer, multi-instrumentalist, main songwriter and decision maker. The line-up on this album, which reached the Top 100 of the US chart, included another brown-skinned lead guitarist John Echols and white boy Bryan Maclean (rhythm guitar and occasional lead vocalist, when Lee allowed it).

Bass player Ken Forssi (ex-Surfaris) had been part of the line-up on their 1966 debut LP, with Alban 'Snoopy' Pfisterer, the drummer on the first LP, on keyboards. Michael Stuart (ex-Sons Of Adam) on drums and Tjay Cantrelli (saxophone) completed the septet.

'Seven And Seven Is' was allegedly written about Lee and a girl friend sharing 7 March as a birthday, and was recorded before Stuart's arrival. Over 20 attempts were needed before the sustained drumming was completed to Lee's satisfaction – after Snoopy, who first tried, became physically exhausted, Lee played the drums himself.

In 1982, Alice Cooper had a UK hit with a cover version of 'Seven And Seven Is'. UK audiences were also

UNREQUITED LOVE

Love never achieved the commercial success critics often predicted. Some feel that their major claim to fame is their indirect responsibility for the discovery of The Doors, the opening act at a show headlined by Love. Elektra founder Jac Holzman saw The Doors for the first time that night, and swiftly signed them.

Love, who had been upstaged by The Doors, produced a worthy follow-up album, Forever Changes, in 1967. By then Snoopy and Cantrelli had departed. Forever Changes was the equal of Da Capo and it was Love's most commercially successful LP in the UK – it peaked outside the Top 150 in the US. By late 1968, the group had broken up.

After leaving Love, Maclean embarked on a solo career, which he soon abandoned, becoming a born-again Christian. Lee recruited a new Love line-up in 1969, but the group's musical direction changed and he and Elektra parted company when Love recorded an album for Blue Thumb Records despite being signed to Elektra. In 1970, on Love's first British tour, Lee recorded an album with Jimi Hendrix, but only one track from this potentially fascinating summit meeting has been released.

familiar with 'The Castle', used as the theme music to a '70s TV series.

US rock act The Hooters covered 'She Comes In Colors' on their 1985 US Top 20 album, *Nervous Night*.

YOUNGER THAN YESTERDAY

THE BYRDS (1967)

SIDE ONE
So You Want To Be A Rock'n'Roll Star
(J. McGuinn/C. Hillman)
Have You Seen Her Face (C. Hillman)
C.T.A. – 102 (J. McGuinn/R. J. Hippard)
Renaissance Fair (D. Crosby/J. McGuinn)
Time Between (C. Hillman)
Everybody's Been Burned (D. Crosby)

SIDE TWO
Thoughts And Words (C. Hillman)
Mind Gardens (D. Crosby)
My Back Pages (B. Dylan)
The Girl With No Name (C. Hillman)
Why (J. McGuinn/D. Crosby)

Produced by Gary Usher
Total running time: 28.31
Released in the US by Columbia Records and in the UK by CBS Records

During the first 18 months of their recording career, US folk/rock group The Byrds had become established stars, with six US Top 50 hit singles and three big-selling albums, *Mr.Tambourine Man*, *Turn! Turn! Turn!* and *Fifth Dimension*.

But after losing original member Gene Clark in early 1966, they needed to silence growing fears that their star was on the wane. Thus this fourth album was vital, and it marked the emergence of vocalist/bass player Chris Hillman as a seasoned and mature songwriter.

The album's first US hit single, 'So You Want To Be A Rock'n'Roll Star', was a sarcastic snipe at overnight stardom, inspired, according to Hillman, by The Monkees – the trumpet part was played by South African jazz star Hugh Masekela, and the screams were taped on the first UK tour by The Byrds.

The album's second US Top 30 hit was a song by Bob Dylan, who had written the group's first two US hit singles, 'Mr.Tambourine Man' and 'All I Really Want To Do'. Hillman was also responsible for the introduction of lead guitarist Clarence White, who played as a session musician on 'Time Between' and 'The Girl With No Name'. In late 1968 he became a full-time Byrd.

Singer/guitarists Jim McGuinn and David Crosby made more predictable songwriting contributions – Crosby's disillusioned 'Everybody's Been Burned' and his ragaesque 'Mind Gardens' seemed obvious progressions from his previous work. McGuinn's spacey 'C.T.A. – 102' achieved the unlikely accolade of being mentioned in an astrophysics magazine.

While their songs were generally regarded as being ambitious if sometimes self-indulgent, Hillman's more straightforward contributions gave the album a balance which made it the most enduring of the group's early output.

SONGBYRDS SUPREME

The Byrds took flight in Los Angeles in 1964. The group was composed of a trio of singer/guitarists. Jim McGuinn had previously worked on the folk circuit in New York's Greenwich Village, and had played guitar on a Judy Collins album. Gene Clark had spent 18 months with folk group The New Christy Minstrels, and David Crosby had been part of ersatz folk combo, Les Baxter's Balladeers.

Crosby was initially (and reluctantly) bass player when the three joined forces, first as The Jet Set and then as The Beefeaters (the name used on their debut single), but when young bluegrass prodigy Chris Hillman joined from The Scotsville Squirrel Barkers on bass, Crosby was free to play rhythm guitar. The final original Byrd, drummer Michael Clarke, had no musical pedigree but was acceptable because his hairstyle was similar to that of Rolling Stone Brian Jones.

THE DOORS

THE DOORS (1967)

SIDE ONE
**Break On Through (To The Other Side)
(The Doors)
Soul Kitchen (The Doors)
The Crystal Ship (The Doors)
Twentieth Century Fox (The Doors)
Alabama Song (Weill/Brecht)
Light My Fire (The Doors)**

SIDE TWO
**Back Door Man (Dixon/Burnett)
I Looked At You (The Doors)
End Of The Night (The Doors)
Take It As It Comes (The Doors)
The End (The Doors)**

*Produced by Paul Rothschild
Total Running Time: 43.25
Released in the US and UK on Elektra Records*

The disappearance and death of vocalist Jim Morrison on 3 July 1971 (coincidentally, the second anniversary of the death of Rolling Stone Brian Jones) finally removed a thorn from the paw of the American establishment which had launched a successful attack on the Doors a year before.

The authorities had thrown the book at Morrison when he supposedly exposed himself onstage. The trouble had started with this, their first album, in 1967, a stunning collection of songs which instantly made the group spokesmen for their generation.

The Doors became instantly immortal among their contemporaries both because of the variety of musical styles they were able to adopt and, possibly more importantly, because the subject matter of their songs had rarely been touched on by rock before that time.

There was R&B: Willie Dixon & Howlin' Wolf's ode to anal penetration, 'Back Door Man'. Berlin theatre was represented by the curious 'Alabama Song (Whisky Bar)' by Bertholdt Brecht & Kurt Weill, which was covered by David Bowie for a single release at the beginning of 1980.

'Twentieth Century Fox' hinted at the group's Hollywood habitat (and the predatory females who hang out there), 'The End' was an Oedipal epic from the fertile mind of Morrison. 'Light My Fire' (later found to be written by guitarist Robbie Krieger) found Morrison in a vibrantly sexy mood.

Morrison's image as the thinking dreamboat with revolution in his sights was in perfect contrast to the studious Ray Manzarek. His quicksilver keyboard skills dominated the group instrumentally; Krieger and drummer John Densmore maintained the momentum.

MONARCH OF THE GLOOMS

Jim Morrison dominates this album even before a note is played. The sleeve pictures present him as a Gulliver among pygmies on the front and in profile on the rear. That mirrored the band's stage act, where the other members were an almost static backdrop to Morrison's antics.

The 'Lizard King' was undoubtedly one of the late 20th Century's most glamorous demi-gods, but he often appeared torn between living up to his 'pretty boy' looks and developing his darker obsessions, as is illustrated by the mix of songs on The Doors.

He eventually destroyed his looks to leave the teenies behind and concentrate on his poetry, but that didn't save him: years of excess ended with his death from a heart attack in a bathtub in Paris, where his grave has become one of rock's more sobering shrines. His behaviour was often childish and indefensible, but his recorded legacy on this timeless album renders his anti-social tendencies irrelevant.

SURREALISTIC PILLOW

JEFFERSON AIRPLANE (1967)

SIDE ONE
She Has Funny Cars
(Jorma Kaukonen/Marty Balin)
Somebody To Love (Darby Slick)
My Best Friend (Skip Spence)
Today (Marty Balin/Paul Kantner)
Comin' Back To Me (Marty Balin)

SIDE TWO
3/5 Of A Mile In 10 Seconds (Marty Balin)
D.C.B.A. – 25 (Paul Kantner)
How Do You Feel (Tom Martin)
Embryonic Journey (Jorma Kaukonen)
White Rabbit (Grace Slick)
Plastic Fantastic Lover (Marty Balin)

Produced by Rick Jarrard
Total running time: 33.37
Released in the US & UK by RCA Records

The first major commercial success of San Francisco's psychedelic explosion (and the trigger for other major labels to sign Bay Area acts), this album reached the US Top 3 and achieved gold status, not least because it included two fine US Top 10 singles, 'Somebody To Love' and 'White Rabbit'.

Formed in 1965 by ex-folkie singer/guitarists Marty Balin and Paul Kantner, the first line-up of the group also included a third local folk singer, Signe Toly Anderson, lead guitarist Jorma Kaukonen, and a rhythm section.

In late 1966, when their debut album *Jefferson Airplane Takes Off* was released, Signe Anderson left, having just become a mother, and the band's male/female vocal blend (a major selling point) was maintained when Kantner suggested offering the job to ex-model Grace Slick.

That became the group's most stable line-up, which was unchanged for over three years, during which time they released five US Top 20 albums.

Slick had previously recorded the two hit singles with The Great Society, a group she fronted which also included her first husband, film-maker Jerry Slick, on drums, and his brother, lead guitarist Darby Slick, who wrote 'Somebody To Love' (recorded in 1965 by The Great Society as 'Someone To Love'). 'White Rabbit' was Grace Slick's brilliant evocation of Lewis Carroll's 'Alice In Wonderland'. These remain Jefferson Airplane's two best-loved recordings.

NAME GAMES

When asked why the group had chosen the name Jefferson, Paul Kantner said: 'We took the J from June, the E from ecstasy, the F from flying, another F from dog, an E from elevator, R from resurrection, S from scintillation, an O from oscillation and a big N from strawberries.'

In early 1970, Dryden left to join The New Riders, and by mid-1972, all the other members of the Surrealistic Pillow line-up had left apart from Slick and Kantner, who had jointly produced a daughter in 1971, whom they named China.

Balin had not contributed to 1970's Blows Against The Empire LP (credited to Paul Kantner & Jefferson Starship) and left to form the short-lived Bodacious D.F., after which he began work on a rock opera which he seems never to have completed.

Kaukonen and Casady launched a splinter group, Hot Tuna (originally Hot Shit, until RCA refused to distribute their eponymous 1970 debut album). The duo finally left Jefferson Airplane when it became Jefferson Starship in early 1974, and continued to record as Hot Tuna.

Airplane's radical approach led to disputes with RCA, who distanced themselves by allowing the group to launch their own label, Grunt Records after Balin left in 1971.

One of London's major rock events of the '60s was Jefferson Airplane's 1968 appearance at London's legendary Roundhouse venue sharing the bill with The Doors.

THE VELVET UNDERGROUND & NICO

THE VELVET UNDERGROUND & NICO (1967)

Produced by Andy Warhol (except 'Sunday Morning', produced by Tom Wilson)
Total running time: 47.52

SIDE ONE
Sunday Morning (Lou Reed)
I'm Waiting For The Man (Lou Reed)
Femme Fatale (Lou Reed)
Venus In Furs (Lou Reed)
Run Run Run (Lou Reed)
All Tomorrow's Parties (Lou Reed)

SIDE TWO
Heroin (Lou Reed)
There She Goes Again (Lou Reed)
I'll Be Your Mirror (Lou Reed)
The Black Angel's Death Song
(Lou Reed/John Cale)
European Son (To Delmore Schwartz)
(Lou Reed/John Cale/Sterling Morrison/
Maureen Tucker)

Released in the US & UK by
Verve Records

Although pop art guru Andy Warhol was involved in many different aspects of '60s popular culture, perhaps his most enduring discovery was The Velvet Underground, whose classic debut album has Warhol's name on the sleeve without any reference to the identity of the group.

Formed in 1964 by the singer/ songwriter/guitarist Lou Reed (real name Louis Firbank) and Welsh music student and multi-instrumentalist John Cale, who recruited the bass player Sterling Morrison and percussionist Angus MacLise, the group adopted their name of The Velvet Underground from a pornographic novel.

As their manager, Warhol introduced German ex-model Nico as 'chanteuse', which alienated MacLise, who swiftly left and was replaced by Maureen Tucker.

By 1966, they were the resident band at Warhol's New York venue, The Factory, becoming part of Warhol's multi-media Exploding Plastic Inevitable extravaganza, and signing to Verve Records, who allowed Warhol to produce this debut album.

Reed's extraordinary songs explored the darker side of the human condition, including drugs ('I'm Waiting For The Man' and 'Heroin'), and sexual fetishism ('Venus In Furs'). The band provided a crunching metallic backing.

The result was hardly pretty music, but its realism starkly contrasted with the peace and love approach of much of the music of the era. Its influence was far-reaching.

PEELING POWER

Soon after this album was released with its peel-off banana skin — the only other words on the front of the sleeve were 'peel slowly and see', with an arrow pointing to the banana, which revealed a pink phallic object – Reed began to call the shots. That resulted in Nico's departure and Warhol's removal by the start of 1968, when the remaining quartet recorded their second LP, White Light, White Heat, in one day. Equally influential and even less of a commercial success, it included such notable songs as the title track, which was admired by David Bowie, 'Sister Ray' and Cale's ultimately bizarre monologue, 'The Gift'. The latter featured Cale telling a strange story about a lovesick person having himself delivered in a large cardboard box to his girlfriend, who is unable to open the box and kills him with industrial wire cutters in her attempts to unwrap it.

After that album, Cale left and was replaced by Doug Yule for a third, eponymous, album in 1969, which failed to chart at all. Their final album, Loaded, was released in 1970. Reed, who by then was on the point of leaving for a solo career, claimed it had been remixed behind his back.

SERGEANT PEPPER'S LONELY HEARTS CLUB BAND

THE BEATLES (1967)

Produced by George Martin
Total running time: 39.52
Released in the UK by Parlophone Records
and in the US by Capitol Records

SIDE ONE

Sgt. Pepper's Lonely Hearts Club Band
(Lennon/McCartney)
With A Little Help From My Friends
(Lennon/McCartney)
Lucy In The Sky With Diamonds
(Lennon/McCartney)
Getting Better (Lennon/McCartney)
Fixing A Hole (Lennon/McCartney)
She's Leaving Home (Lennon/McCartney)
Being For The Benefit of Mr. Kite
(Lennon/McCartney)

SIDE TWO

Within You Without You (Harrison)
When I'm Sixty-Four (Lennon/McCartney)
Lovely Rita (Lennon/McCartney)
Good Morning Good Morning
(Lennon/McCartney)
Sgt. Pepper's Lonely Hearts Club Band
(Reprise) (Lennon/McCartney)
A Day In The Life (Lennon/McCartney)

For The Beatles, the most popular group in the world, 1967 was a watershed year, of which *Sergeant Pepper*, the finest album of the entire rock era, was a major ingredient.

The quartet, who had abandoned touring in 1966, had become bored with their new-found freedom. Thus their eighth original album presented a fresh challenge which, helped by producer George Martin, they eagerly accepted.

It was Paul McCartney who suggested that it should resemble a live recording by a fictional band, and the absence of physical indications of where a track started and ended was one more example of their pioneering spirit, as was their use of the back of the sleeve for printing each song's lyrics.

A new Beatles album provided others who covered its songs with near certain hits. This was no exception: Joe Cocker's radical revival of 'With A Little Help From My Friends' (sung here by Ringo, aka 'Billy Shears') topped the UK chart a year later, and Elton John's live 'Lucy In The Sky' (with John Lennon, who was keeping a promise) was a 1974 hit.

But the definitive versions of the title track, the much-discussed 'A Day In The Life' and other songs here are these originals. The McCartney-inspired 'She's Leaving Home' (without George and Ringo, replaced by string players and including a harp) and 'When I'm 64' were brilliant, if soft-centred.

Lennon's 'Mr.Kite' and 'Good Morning' lacked melody. Clearly, the collaboration between the group's two main writers was ending.

George Harrison was allowed to do an Indian-styled song, 'Within You Without You', placed at the start of side two (perhaps so that it could be easily skipped), but the advent of the CD partially eliminated this user-friendliness.

Ironic, then, that the oft-heard excuse for not buying a CD player was 'Not until *Sergeant Pepper*'s on CD.'

Sergeant Pepper even returned to the Top 3 of the UK album chart when the CD version finally emerged in 1987 to mark the 20th anniversary of its release.

THE RECORDING

As well as expanding the consciousness of its listeners, Sergeant Pepper's Lonely Hearts Club Band *set new creative targets for The Beatles' contemporaries.*

It took up almost 700 hours of studio time; The Beatles allegedly spent many of those hours high on LSD. With the band sometimes incapable of production, George Martin did a superb job, accommodating instruments unfamiliar to those on the rock scene and working wonders with tape mixes. The result was a perfect mixture of the exotic and the English.

ELECTRIC MUSIC FOR THE MIND AND BODY
COUNTRY JOE & THE FISH (1967)

Produced by: Sam Charters
Total running time: 44.18
Released in the US & the UK by Vanguard Records

 oe McDonald personified the radical revolutionary aspect of late '60s rock and this superb debut album is a classic example of '60s drugs and protest music.

McDonald, born on 1 January 1942, was named after Russian dictator Joseph Stalin by his communist-sympathising parents. In 1964, he moved to Berkeley, California, an area near San Francisco noted for its radical politics and large student population.

This album includes two songs that had featured on his first recording, a 1965 EP: 'Super Bird' (a political barb aimed at US President Lyndon Johnson) and 'I Feel Like I'm Fixing To Die Rag'.

A student magazine gave McDonald and cohorts the name Country Joe & The Fish (a reference to something said by Chairman Mao, the Chinese dictator).

Among the more daring tracks here are the reputedly drug-influenced 'Bass Strings' and a lengthy instrumental, 'Section 43'.

For this album, Country Joe & The Fish, who had metamorphosed from acoustic jug band to psychedelic electric group, re-recorded three songs from earlier EPs. The other eight tracks were originals, including 'Flying High', a classic drug anthem, and the Bob Dylan-influenced 'Not So Sweet Martha Lorraine' (the band's only US chart single). The LP reached the US Top 40 during a nine month chart run, but it was less successful in the UK.

SIDE ONE
Flying High (Joe McDonald/Barry Melton, David Cohen/Bruce Barthol/Gary Hirsh)
Not So Sweet Martha Lorraine (Joe McDonald/Barry Melton/ David Cohen/Bruce Barthol/Gary Hirsh)
Death Sound (Joe McDonald/Barry Melton/ David Cohen/Bruce Barthol/Gary Hirsh)
Porpoise Mouth (Joe McDonald/ Barry Melton/David Cohen/ Bruce Barthol/Gary Hirsh)
Section 43 (Joe McDonald/Barry Melton/ David Cohen/Bruce Barthol/Gary Hirsh)

SIDE TWO
Super Bird (Joe McDonald/Barry Melton/ David Cohen/Bruce Barthol/Gary Hirsh)
Sad And Lonely Times (Joe McDonald/ Barry Melton/David Cohen/ Bruce Barthol/Gary Hirsh)
Love (Joe McDonald/Barry Melton/ David Cohen/Bruce Barthol/Gary Hirsh)
Bass Strings (Joe McDonald/ Barry Melton/David Cohen/ Bruce Barthol/Gary Hirsh)
The Masked Marauder (Joe McDonald/ Barry Melton/David Cohen/ Bruce Barthol/Gary Hirsh)
Grace (Joe McDonald/Barry Melton/ David Cohen/Bruce Barthol/Gary Hirsh)

FISHY SPELLING

Joe McDonald made his first recording in 1964 with a friend, Blair Hardman. But only 200 copies of the LP they made were pressed. By 1967, he was a familiar figure around San Francisco and wrote songs about other local stars such as 'Grace' on this album (Grace Slick, later of Jefferson Airplane) and 'Janis' on the group's second album, I Feel Like I'm Fixin' To Die (dedicated to Janis Joplin).

The title track of this second album was a re-recording of another track from his first EP, McDonald's anti-war song about Vietnam, which was preceded by something known as 'The Fish Cheer', an audience participation item in which McDonald instructs the crowd to 'Gimme an F', 'Gimme an I', etc., ending with 'What's that spell?' to which the response is 'Fish'. However, the four letter word beginning with F which was spelt out was not always Fish.

THE PIPER AT THE GATES OF DAWN

PINK FLOYD (1967)

SIDE ONE
Astronomy Domine (Barrett)
Lucifer Sam (Barrett)
Matilda Mother (Barrett)
Flaming (Barrett)
Pow R. Toc H.
(Barrett/Waters/Wright/Mason)
Take Up Thy Stethoscope And Walk
(Waters)

SIDE TWO
Interstellar Overdrive
(Barrett/Waters/Wright/Mason)
The Gnome (Barrett)
Chapter 24 (Barrett)
The Scarecrow (Barrett)
Bike (Barrett)

Produced by Norman Smith
Total running time: 41.58
Released in the UK by EMI/Columbia Records and in the US by Tower Records
The US release omitted 'Astronomy Domine', 'Flaming' and 'Bike', and included 'See Emily Play'

Pink Floyd were one of Britain's first genuinely psychedelic groups, formed in late 1965, when three students of architecture, drummer Nick Mason, bass player Roger Waters and Rick Wright (keyboards), were joined by singer/ guitarist Roger 'Syd' Barrett, a schoolfriend of Waters from Cambridge.

Barrett was the group's main songwriter. He wrote their first two singles, 'Arnold Layne' (about a thief who stole female underwear from washing lines) and 'See Emily Play' (originally titled 'Games For May' and written as the theme song for a 1967 concert at London's Queen Elizabeth Hall). Both were sizeable UK hits.

This debut album, titled after a chapter in Kenneth Grahame's classic children's book, 'Wind In The Willows', again predominantly featured Barrett songs, which are often puzzling and obscure.

The opening riff of 'Interstellar Overdrive' (one of two tracks here previewing the group's later musical direction of the long, 'spacey' instrumental, the other being 'Astronomy Domine') was supposedly copied from Love's first hit, 'My Little Red Book'.

The inspiration behind 'Chapter 24' was the 'I Ching', a Chinese fortune-telling book. 'Lucifer Sam' names Barrett's girlfriend in Cambridge, Jenny, and the Tolkienesque 'The Gnome' was a typical nonsensical Barrett lyric.

One reviewer suggested that the 'Stethoscope' song by Waters had actually been written by bluesman Muddy Waters...

THE FLOYD'S CRAZY DIAMOND

Syd Barrett (top right in the neo-psychedelic sleeve photograph) was certainly a genius, but his much-publicised dabbling with mind-expanding drugs seemed to release a mental instability from which he had yet to recover, over 25 years later.

After this album was released, Barrett grew increasingly distant and unreliable, to the point where it was decided to invite Dave Gilmour to join as a guitarist. The five piece Pink Floyd (named, incidentally, after two obscure US bluesmen, Floyd Council and Pink Anderson) lasted five shows before Barrett was eased out of the band after contributing to three tracks on A Saucerful Of Secrets, in 1968. He eventually embarked on a brief solo career which produced two albums, The Madcap Laughs and Barrett, both released in 1970. Since then, despite not recording anything of note, Barrett has become legendary, with numerous tributes in the form of fanzines, a best-selling biography, and many cover versions of his songs, as well as songs inspired by him, notably 'Shine On You Crazy Diamond' from Pink Floyd's 1975 chart-topping album, Wish You Were Here.

GREATEST HITS

THE FOUR TOPS (1967)

Produced by Brian Holland & Lamont Dozier, except * (by Ivy Hunter), ** (by William Stevenson & Ivy Hunter)
Total running time: 44.40
Released in the US by Motown Records and in the UK by Tamla Motown Records
The US release omits 'Where Did You Go', 'You Keep Running Away', 'Darling, I Hum Our Song' and 'I'll Turn To Stone'

SIDE ONE
Reach Out I'll Be There
(Holland/Dozier/Holland)
Where Did You Go
(Holland/Dozier/Holland)
I Can't Help Myself
(Holland/Dozier/Holland)
Seven Rooms Of Gloom
(Holland/Dozier/Holland)
Loving You Is Sweeter Than Ever
(Hunter/Wonder) *
Standing In The Shadows Of Love
(Holland/Dozier/Holland)
Something About You
(Holland/Dozier/Holland)
Baby I Need Your Loving
(Holland/Dozier/Holland)

SIDE TWO
You Keep Running Away
(Holland/Dozier/Holland)
Shake Me, Wake Me (When It's Over)
(Holland/Dozier/Holland)
Ask The Lonely (Hunter/Stevenson) **
Bernadette (Holland/Dozier/Holland)
Darling, I Hum Our Song
(Holland/Dozier/Holland)
Without The One You Love (Life's Not Worth While) (Holland/Dozier/Holland)
It's The Same Old Song
(Holland/Dozier/Holland)
I'll Turn To Stone
(Holland/Dozier/Holland/DeVol)

The Supremes were the first Motown group to hit the big time in Britain; their male equivalent was The Four Tops. This splendid collection topped the UK chart in early 1968, and was in fact knocked off the Number 1 slot by the equivalent *Greatest Hits* LP by The Supremes. In their native US, it is the only Four Tops album to have reached the Top 10.

These achievements were well-deserved. This was a genuine *Greatest Hits*, with the US version including the group's 12 US Top 50 hits up to and including 'Seven Rooms Of Gloom' in mid-1967. Two chart-toppers: 'I Can't Help Myself' and 'Reach Out I'll Be There', were included, as were three more which reached the Top 10: 'It's The Same Old Song', 'Standing In The Shadows Of Love' and 'Bernadette'.

In the UK, the success was slightly less sensational, although 'Reach Out' was the group's first Number 1, while seven of the others were hits.

Most of these timeless hits were written by brothers Brian & Eddie Holland with Lamont Dozier, who also produced them with Brian Holland. What makes this achievement even more spectacular is that during the same three year period, the HDH team also wrote and produced ten US Number 1 hits for The Supremes!

TOP THAT!

The Four Tops are the longest standing group of the rock era. They formed in 1953 (as The Four Aims), and remained in operation (if slightly less sprightly) in the mid-'90s!

With an unchanged line-up of Levi Stubbs (lead vocalist) supported by backing singers Abdul 'Duke' Fakir, Renaldo 'Obie' Benson and Lawrence Payton, all from Detroit, Michigan (the home of the Ford Motor Company, the Motortown which gave the Motown label its name), the quartet met at a party and decided to join forces.

For ten years, the group were unsuccessful as recording artists, recording for five labels during an eight-year spell without even reaching the US R&B chart, let alone the pop chart. It wasn't until 1964 that they had their first hit, 'Baby I Need Your Loving' on Motown.

GREATEST HITS

DIANA ROSS & THE SUPREMES (1968)

Produced by Brian Holland, Lamont Dozier &
Eddie Holland
Total running time: 45.32
Released in the UK on Tamla Motown Records

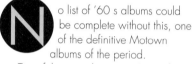

SIDE ONE
Stop! In The Name Of Love
(Holland/Dozier/Holland)
Nothing But Heartaches
(Holland/Dozier/Holland)
**When The Lovelight Starts Shining Thru
His Eyes** (Holland/Dozier/Holland)
My World Is Empty Without You
(Holland/Dozier/Holland)
Where Did Our Love Go
(Holland/Dozier/Holland)
Love Is Like An Itching In My Heart
(Holland/Dozier/Holland)
Come See About Me
(Holland/Dozier/Holland)
I Hear A Symphony
(Holland/Dozier/Holland)

SIDE TWO
Reflections (Holland/Dozier/Holland)
Back In My Arms Again
(Holland/Dozier/Holland)
You Keep Me Hanging On
(Holland/Dozier/Holland)
Whisper You Love Me Boy
(Holland/Dozier/Holland)
The Happening (De Vol)
Love Is Here And Now You're Gone
(Holland/Dozier/Holland)
You Can't Hurry Love
(Holland/Dozier/Holland)
Baby Love (Holland/Dozier/Holland)

N o list of '60 s albums could be complete without this, one of the definitive Motown albums of the period.

Ten of these tracks were US Number 1s in under three years and 11 were UK hits, making Diana Ross, Florence Ballard and Mary Wilson the hottest black act in the world between 1964, when 'Where Did Our Love Go' first enchanted the world, and 1967.

The earliest track, 1963's 'When The Lovelight Starts Shining Thru His Eyes', was their first US Top 30 hit. The others, except 'Whisper You Love Me Boy' and 'Back In My Arms Again', made the US Top 10, and are among the most frequently heard 'oldies' of the era.

Following a series of commercial flops, a change in the trio's fortunes came when Berry Gordy instructed Ross to take over as lead vocalist from Ballard, which pleased Ross and devastated Ballard. Removed from the group in 1967, she slid into personal and artistic decline and died penniless in 1976, aged just 32.

The group's name was changed to reflect Ross's pre-eminence and the big hits continued until 1969, when she left the group for a solo career.

MOTOWN'S PRIME STARS

Previously known as The Primettes (the 'sister' group to The Primes, who evolved into The Temptations, just as The Primettes evolved when given their new name). The Supremes were initially a quartet until Barbara Martin left in 1961. After signing with Motown that year, their first five single releases during their first three years at Motown were unsuccessful. Their most notable achievement before 1964 was being backing vocalists on Marvin Gaye's 'Can I Get A Witness'.

As soon as they were assigned to the Holland, Dozier & Holland team, things totally changed, and, during the middle of the decade, no other female act approached their international popularity, which rivalled that of every contemporary act other than The Beatles.

One of the more unlikely cover versions of one of their ten Number 1 hits was white hard rock quartet Vanilla Fudge's 'You Keep Me Hangin' On', which was a big hit in 1968. Their ponderously heavy slowed down arrangement came as a total contrast to the urgent plea of the original by The Supremes.

BUFFALO SPRINGFIELD AGAIN

BUFFALO SPRINGFIELD (1968)

SIDE ONE
Mr. Soul (Neil Young)
A Child's Claim To Fame (Richie Furay)
Everydays (Steve Stills)
Expecting To Fly (Neil Young)
Bluebird (Steve Stills)

SIDE TWO
Hung Upside Down (Steve Stills)
Bad Memory (Richie Furay)
Good Time Boy (Richie Furay)
Rock & Roll Woman (Steve Stills)
Broken Arrow (Neil Young)

Produced by: Neil Young, Richie Furay, Steve Stills, Charlie Greene & Brian Stone, Jack Nitzsche, Ahmet Ertegun, Dewey Martin

Total running time: 33.58
Released in the US by Atco Records and in the UK by Atlantic Records

Buffalo Springfield didn't last long as a group, but for this album, despite its fragmented qualities, they remain revered.

Singer/guitarists Steve (later Stephen) Stills from Texas and Richie Furay from Ohio became friends in New York when both were in a folk cabaret group, The Au Gogo Singers.

When he saw the first Beatles movie, 'A Hard Day's Night', Stills knew he had to be in a rock group and moved to California. Furay also moved west, and they began writing songs, but it wasn't until they were stuck in a traffic jam on Sunset Boulevard that things began to happen. On the other side of the road was a hearse with Canadian number plates, containing Neil Young, a singer/songwriter whose work they had admired on the New York folk circuit, and bass player Bruce Palmer, who were looking for Stills and Furay in the hope of joining their band.

With drummer Dewey Martin, the group made an eponymous debut album and scored a US Top 10 single with a protest song written by Stills, 'For What It's Worth'.

This second album rarely featured the same line-up on any two tracks – three bass players, a dobro, a banjo, a grand piano, were all played by different people. Yet the result is delightful, and three US hit singles are included: 'Bluebird' and 'Rock'n'Roll Woman', both by Stills, and the exotic 'Expecting To Fly', a third Neil Young masterpiece alongside 'Mr.Soul' and 'Broken Arrow'.

DRUG PROBLEMS

One of the reasons for the group's unsettled line-up was that Bruce Palmer ran foul of the law and was deported twice for minor drug offences and once for illegally entering the US.

He was at one point replaced by Jim Fielder, who later became a founder member of Blood, Sweat & Tears, and by several other short-staying musicians, and as the group came to the end of its life, by Jim Messina (later of Loggins & Messina).

Neil Young left and rejoined Buffalo Springfield several times during their two year life, constantly quarrelling with his colleagues.

But it was Richie Furay who became the first to form a post-Springfield group, Poco, which also included Jim Messina, Randy Meisner, who worked with Rick Nelson's Stone Canyon Band and who was later a founder member of The Eagles, and Rusty Young, a brilliant pedal steel player.

Furay later attempted a solo career before deciding to become a clergyman (a career for which his life as a rock musician can hardly have prepared him).

Stills played on Al Kooper's Super Session album before joining David Crosby (ex-The Byrds) and Graham Nash (ex-Hollies) in Crosby, Stills & Nash in late 1968.

DAYS OF FUTURE PASSED

THE MOODY BLUES WITH THE LONDON FESTIVAL ORCHESTRA (1968)

SIDE ONE
The Day Begins (Redwave/Knight)
Dawn Is A Feeling (Pinder)
Another Morning (Thomas)
Peak Hour (Lodge)

SIDE TWO
Forever Afternoon (Tuesday?) (Hayward)
(Evening) Time To Get Away (Lodge)
The Sun Set (Pinder)
Twilight Time (Thomas)
Nights In White Satin (Hayward)

Produced by Tony Clarke
Total running time: 41.47
Released in the UK and the US by
Deram Records

By mid-1966, Birmingham quintet The Moody Blues, who had topped the UK singles chart in early 1965 with 'Go Now', were in what appeared to be terminal decline after Denny Laine (vocals, guitar) and Clint Warwick (bass) had left the band.

The other three founder members, Mike Pinder (keyboards), Ray Thomas (flute, vocals) and Graeme Edge (drums), recruited vocalist/guitarist Justin Hayward and vocalist/bassist John Lodge as replacements, but the group seemed doomed despite the new blood.

Decca were unwilling to let them record again after three singles flopped in early 1967 but fate intervened. Decca, who also sold hi-fi equipment, needed a demonstration LP to showcase its Deramic sound system. They decided to record Dvorak's 'New World Symphony' with orchestral backing.

The job was offered to The Moody Blues, who were on the verge of breaking up, but they accepted the offer as they had nothing else in view.

The idea of the Dvorak symphony was quickly abandoned in favour of recording this concept album of original songs about different times of the day.

Released at the end of 1967, it entered the UK chart after 'Nights In White Satin' became a UK hit single, which led it to the US album chart.

The first US hit from the album was 'Tuesday Afternoon (Forever Afternoon)' (a slight title change), which reached the US Top 30.

'Nights In White Satin' was not released as a single in the US until 1972, when it sold a million copies and reached the US Top 3. After that it was reissued in the UK and reached the Top 10. Even so, the album has never reached the Top 20 of the UK chart.

A SECURE FUTURE

Days Of Future Passed was the first in a succession of internationally successful albums by The Moody Blues from 1967 until 1972, when the group decided to take a sabbatical. In Search Of The Lost Chord (1968) was a bigger hit in the UK, where it reached the Top 5, than in the US, as was their first album of 1969, On The Threshold Of A Dream, which not only inspired the name of the group's own label, Threshold Records, but also topped the UK chart. The same year also produced To Our Children's Children's Children, which made the UK Top 3, and was their first album since Days Of Future Passed to reach the US Top 20.

The run continued with A Question Of Balance (1970, UK Number 1, US Top 3), Every Good Boy Deserves Favour (1971, UK Number 1, US Top 3) and Seventh Sojourn (1972, US Number 1, UK Top 5), after which each member of the group concentrated on individual projects. During the six years when the group was inactive, the only members who were successful were Justin Hayward and John Lodge, who joined forces in 1975 and released an album with the cleverly chosen title of Blue Jays, which reached the Top 10 of the UK chart.

SELL OUT

THE WHO (1968)

THE WHO SELL OUT

Replacing the stale smell of excess with the sweet smell of success, Peter Townshend, who, like nine out of ten stars, needs it. Face the music with "Odorono", the all-day deodorant that turns perspiration into inspiration.

THE WHO SELL OUT

This way to a cowboy's breakfast. Daltrey rides again. Thanks: "Thanks to Heinz Baked Beans everyday is a super day." Those who know how many beans make five get Heinz beans inside and outside at every opportunity. Get saucy.

SIDE ONE

Armenia City In The Sky (John Keen)
Heinz Baked Beans (John Entwistle)
Mary Anne With The Shaky Hand
(Pete Townshend)
Odorono (Pete Townshend)
Tattoo (Pete Townshend)
Our Love Was (Pete Townshend)
I Can See For Miles (Pete Townshend)

SIDE TWO

Can't Reach You (Pete Townshend)
Medac (John Entwistle)
Relax (Pete Townshend)
Silas Stingy (John Entwistle)
Sunrise (Pete Townshend)
Rael (1 & 2) (Pete Townshend)

Produced by Kit Lambert
Total running time: 39.44
Released in the UK by Track Records and in the US by Decca Records

For The Who's third album, Pete Townshend came up with some straightforward (and excellent) songs.

These included 'I Can See For Miles' (a Top 10 single on both sides of the Atlantic), 'Armenia' and 'Our Love Was'.

Townshend also used authentic radio commercials used by the offshore pirate station, Radio London, plus original commercials and songs for well-known products of the time.

This inspired the eye-catching album sleeve, picturing Townshend with a giant stick deodorant in his armpit (relating to the track 'Odorono') and singer Roger Daltrey enjoying a bath of 'Heinz Baked Beans' (perhaps inspiring the sequence in the 'Tommy' movie in which the Swedish film star Ann-Margret undergoes a similar experience).

'Medac' (titled 'Spotted Henry' on the US version of the album) tells the story of Henry Pond who has a complexion like a currant bun (although Keith Moon portrays him on the sleeve as having an Olympic-qualifying birthmark) and John Entwistle as the seven stone weakling who has subscribed to a Charles Atlas body-building course, enabling him to get the blonde in the leopard-skin bikini with whom he's pictured.

The album reflects Townshend's desire to strike a blow for pirate radio, a *cause celebre* in the UK at the time, which had resulted in the opening of a national (and legal) pop radio network, BBC Radio One. *The Who Sell Out* remains a piece of history, especially in the UK.

MILES BETTER

'I Can See For Miles' was The Who's breakthrough US single, but was viewed in the UK as a comparative failure, particularly as Townshend had written it some time before and recorded a home demo which was at least as exciting as anything he had done previously.

It was a similar story as far as the UK and US album charts were concerned – both their debut LP, My Generation, and their follow-up, A Quick One (While He's Away) (titled Happy Jack in the US) had made the Top 10 of the UK album chart, but neither had reached the Top 50 of the US chart.

The lack of synchronisation between the group's UK and US releases resulted from their being signed to unconnected labels – Track Records was a brand new UK company formed by The Who's managers, Kit Lambert & Chris Stamp, while Decca, a US corporation in operation since the '20s, had signed The Who through a production deal between their first record producer, Shel Talmy, and Brunswick Records, Decca's UK subsidiary. While the group's contract with Talmy and Brunswick could be terminated, it was less easy to end their ties to Decca (later MCA), to whom the group remained contracted throughout the '70s.

JOHN WESLEY HARDING

BOB DYLAN (1968)

SIDE ONE
John Wesley Harding (B. Dylan)
As I Went Out One Morning (B. Dylan)
I Dreamed I Saw St.Augustine (B. Dylan)
All Along The Watchtower (B. Dylan)
The Ballad Of Frankie Lee And Judas
Priest (B. Dylan)
Drifter's Escape (B. Dylan)

SIDE TWO
Dear Landlord (B. Dylan)
I Am A Lonesome Hobo (B. Dylan)
I Pity The Poor Immigrant (B. Dylan)
The Wicked Messenger (B. Dylan)
Down Along The Cove (B. Dylan)
I'll Be Your Baby Tonight (B. Dylan)

Produced by Bob Johnston
Total tunning time: 38.32

Released in the US by Columbia Records
and in the UK by CBS Records

he Indians on the front of the sleeve are The Bauls Of Bengal, but more significant was that this was Dylan's first LP since his motorcycle accident.

Maybe like everyone else in times of panic, he had become aware of his mortality, and was using his fame to broadcast his thanks for being spared. Or maybe he had found answers, or at least clues, in his quest for enlightenment from fundamentalist religion, even if the start of 'I Dreamed I Saw St. Augustine' is apparently lyrically similar to an older song written about an early American trade unionist, Joe Hill.

The big songs on the album are 'All Along The Watchtower', transformed by Jimi Hendrix into a quite different song and a memorable hit, and 'I'll Be Your Baby Tonight', an instantly familiar song which has been covered by loads of acts on albums, but seems never to have been a hit single. A very straightforward love song (in contrast to 'Watchtower', which has all the attributes of his 'mystical' past classics), it's quite typical of the album as a whole, which is emphatically non-electric.

The sound is gentle overall, which makes it ironic that one of the heaviest metal bands of the '70s, Judas Priest, was named after the neo-religious morality tale also involving 'Frankie Lee', which seems to be about being helpful to others and renouncing lust.

A small band, a trio most of the time, with Charlie McCoy on bass and Kenny Buttrey on drums (both from the *Blonde On Blonde* recordings) plus Dylan, and a third Nashville cat, steel guitarist Pete Drake, on the last two tracks, provided at least some contrast to an album style that frequently consists of a short instrumental intro, a vocal of several verses without instrumental punctuation, and a final flurry on the harmonica in familiarly flamboyant Dylan style.

Did he write 'Down Along The Cove' so that Elvis Presley might cover it as a musical relative to 'Mystery Train'? We may never know.

A TROUBADOR ON THE MOVE

This was the start of the third major direction taken by Dylan in the '60s. Inside seven years he had metamorphosed from the Woody Guthrie-esque phase through the tough electric rock of 'Like A Rolling Stone' to country singer/songwriter. The Nashville direction continued for his final original album of the decade, Nashville Skyline, with Johnny Cash duetting on 'Girl From The North Country', and more gentle songs, including the classic 'Lay, Lady, Lay'.

In the summer of 1969, Dylan dipped into his past (as he had done by appearing at a 1968 memorial concert for Woody Guthrie at Carnegie Hall in New York) by appearing at the Isle Of Wight Festival in the UK backed by The Band, arguably the only backing group he trusted to support him.

BOOGIE WITH CANNED HEAT

CANNED HEAT (1968)

SIDE ONE
Evil Woman (Larry Weiss)
My Crime (Canned Heat)
On The Road Again (Shade/Jones)
World In A Jug (Canned Heat)
Turpentine Moan (Canned Heat)
Whiskey Headed Woman No. 2 (Hite Jr.)

SIDE TWO
Amphetamine Annie (Hite Jr.)
An Owl Song (Wilson)
Marie Laveau (Vestine)
Fried Hockey Boogie (Taylor)

Produced by Dallas Smith
Total running time: 44.32
Released in the US & The UK by Liberty Records

Californian country blues enthusiasts Canned Heat rocketed to fame with this memorable second album (their biggest ever, a whole year in the US chart), which included their first US Top 20 single, 'On The Road Again'.

Formed by blues scholars Bob 'The Bear' Hite (vocals) and Al 'Blind Owl' Wilson (vocals, harmonica, slide guitar) with lead guitarist Henry 'Sun' Vestine (ex-Mothers Of Invention) and bass player Larry 'Mole' Taylor (who had appeared as a session musician on early hits by The Monkees), the group featured drummer Adopho 'Fito' De La Parra for the first time here.

Apart from the hit single, it included another notable track in 'Fried Hockey Boogie' (11 minutes plus), the first recorded appearance of an insistent bass riff which would become a major feature of the group's live work, when it was used as a platform for (sometimes over-) lengthy soloing.

The group's next album, *Living The Blues* (a 2xLP set also released in 1968), included an over-extended (almost 40 minutes) version of this tune titled 'Refried Boogie' taking up both sides of one complete LP.

The group's decline was clearly due to the big-hearted and avuncular Hite's onstage vocal dominance, while the first two (and biggest) hit singles featured Wilson singing lead in his unique falsetto. At the start it didn't matter a great deal (as proved by the group's triumphant appearance at the 1969 Woodstock Festival), but Vestine's departure in 1969, followed by

Wilson's death (reputedly of a drug overdose) in the autumn of 1970, left a yawning gap which replacements (even noted Chicago guitarist Harvey Mandel) were unable to totally fill.

CANNED MUSIC

Canned Heat (a name that had been appropriated from a record by an obscure bluesman, Tommy Johnson, 'Canned Heat Blues') almost single-handedly flew the country blues flag during the '60s.

The varied influences in the group (Frank Zappa to Jerry Lee Lewis, with whom Taylor had played before Canned Heat, along with the scholarly expertise of Wilson, who studied music at college, and Hite, who worked in a record shop specialising in blues 78s) led to relatively narrow musical horizons, although Vestine's 'Marie Laveau' owed something to cajun influence.

However, the chemistry between the larger-than-life Hite and his short-sighted, introverted co-founder, Wilson, might have enabled the group to survive, had not Wilson's manic depressive tendencies led to his early death.

As it was, Bob Hite kept the Heat more or less on the boil until he also died in 1981, from a reputedly drug-related heart attack, although many felt that the excessive body weight he had carried for most of his life may have played at least as big a part as any drug.

FLEETWOOD MAC

PETER GREEN'S FLEETWOOD MAC (1968)

SIDE ONE
My Heart Beat Like A Hammer (J. Spencer)
Merry Go Round (P. A. Green)
Long Grey Mare (P. A. Green)
Hellhound On My Trail
(Trad. arr. P. A. Green)
Shake Your Moneymaker (E. James)
Looking For Somebody (P. A. Green)

SIDE TWO
No Place To Go (C. Burnett)
My Baby's Good To Me (J. Spencer)
I Loved Another Woman (P. A. Green)
Cold Black Night (J. Spencer)
The World Keeps On Turning (P. A. Green)
Got To Move (Homesick James Williamson)

Produced by Mike Vernon
Total running time: 34.20
Released in the UK by Blue Horizon Records and in the US by Epic Records

In early 1968, Fleetwood Mac made this first LP, which is an interesting mix of tunes by famous US bluesmen and homegrown British blues.

Fleetwood Mac first formed in 1967 when singer/guitarist Green and drummer Mick Fleetwood left John Mayall's Bluesbreakers.

They called the new band that they assembled Fleetwood Mac (but succumbed to pressure to use Green's name as a preface). Slide guitarist Elmore James was vocalist/guitarist Jeremy Spencer's particular hero – and James's 'Shake Your Moneymaker' had also been included on the 1965 debut LP by Paul Butterfield's Blues Band.

Other majestic blues figures to have their work covered on this album included Howlin' Wolf (aka Chester Burnett) and Homesick James.

The original compositions by Green could also be traced clearly to their origins, such as the Howlin' Wolf-like 'No Place To Go' and the country blues of 'The World Keeps On Turning'.

Spencer could also produce infinite variations on the famed Elmore James guitar riff of 'Dust My Broom' which were very much inspired and influenced by the blues, as was the sleeve picture. One track, 'Long Grey Mare', comes from the group's first recording session and features Bob Brunning, the group's first bass player, although he was soon replaced by John McVie, another recruit from John Mayall's Bluesbreakers.

McVie had initially elected to stay with Mayall, for reasons of financial stability, but he was fired soon afterwards, and then decided that joining Peter Green and Fleetwood Mac was a good idea after all.

The album was an instant hit in the UK, reaching the Top 5 of the album chart, but only just making the bottom of the US Top 200.

A CONTROVERSIAL COVER

The sleeve photo of Fleetwood Mac's second album, Mr. Wonderful, featured Mick Fleetwood naked but for a few strategically placed bits of foliage. It was intrepid but unnecessarily controversial – according to a biographer, the group had originally titled the album A Good Length, but taste eventually prevailed.

At this point, the band expanded by recruiting yet another singer/guitarist, 18-year-old Danny Kirwan, from Boilerhouse, a smalltime blues group which had supported Fleetwood Mac in 1967. Kirwan's first appearance on record with the group came with 'Albatross', an uncharacteristic instrumental by Green surprisingly similar in style to The Shadows. It also surprised Fleetwood Mac, although in a very pleasant manner, as it topped the UK singles chart in early 1969, and re-entered the UK Top 3 in 1973 when it was reissued.

THE SONGS OF LEONARD COHEN

LEONARD COHEN (1968)

SIDE ONE
Suzanne (L. Cohen)
Master Song (L. Cohen)
Winter Lady (L. Cohen)
The Stranger Song (L. Cohen)
Sisters Of Mercy (L. Cohen)

SIDE TWO
So Long, Marianne (L. Cohen)
Hey, That's No Way To Say Goodbye
(L. Cohen)
Stories Of The Street (L. Cohen)
Teachers (L. Cohen)
One Of Us Cannot Be Wrong (L. Cohen)

Produced by John Simon
Total running time: 41.14

Released in the US on Columbia Records
and in the UK on CBS Records

Leonard Cohen was (and, in the '90s remained) a genuinely sensitive artist, with little ambition to become a star, preferring his privacy and solitude to public fame.

His finest songs, and several of them appear here, are timeless examples of poetry inspired by tragic love affairs.

A Canadian singer/songwriter whose lyrics did justice to the label placed on him of 'singing poet', was in his mid-thirties when this first album was released. It reached the Top 100 of the US album chart, and was his only early album to achieve gold status for 500,000 sales.

The honest recipe of Cohen's mournful delivery of his equally mournful songs touched a nerve, particularly among young females, who found him sensitive and sadly resigned, a perfect fantasy lover who they might never meet, but whose songs were beautifully poetic.

Those songs were usually crafted in an intense emotional forge, while the tragic sepia photograph on the album sleeve added to the effect, with its portrayal of a man of sorrows acquainted with grief who had a resemblance to Oscar Wilde and other 19th Century literary celebrities.

The best-known songs here are 'Suzanne', 'Sisters Of Mercy' and 'Hey, That's No Way To Say Goodbye', all of which have attracted cover versions by notable artists, including Judy Collins, who recorded all three, Dion, Roberta Flack and Joan Baez.

AN URBANE POET

Born in 1934, Leonard Cohen's first book of poetry, 'Let Us Compare Mythologies', was published in 1956. His first performances were in pre-rock beatnik style, reciting his poetry accompanied by a jazz pianist, but after an attempt at setting his poems to music failed to interest music publishers, he reverted to writing straightforward poetry, and a second book, 'The Spice-Box Of Earth', was published in 1961.

In the '60s, he wrote two novels, 'The Favourite Game' (1963) and the acclaimed 'Beautiful Losers' (1966), as well as two more volumes of poetry, 'Flowers For Hitler' (1964) and 'Parasites Of Heaven' (1966). In the latter year, he again tried to turn his poems into songs, achieving success when Judy Collins included 'Suzanne' on her album, In My Life.

After the release of his second album, Songs From A Room, Cohen spent nearly two years performing live in Europe, where he could more easily enjoy his Jacques Brel-like status, and appeared at the 1970 Isle Of Wight Festival.

Cohen's talent as a songwriter is to capture his extreme vulnerability to romance, and his helplessness in the face of being in love. His mature and usually witty use of language adds an extra dimension to his suicidal lyrical approach.

CHILD IS FATHER TO THE MAN

BLOOD, SWEAT & TEARS (1968)

Produced by John Simon
Total running time: 49.39
Released in the US by Columbia Records and in the UK by CBS Records

SIDE ONE
Overture (Al Kooper)
I Love You More Than You'll Ever Know
(Al Kooper)
Morning Glory (Tim Buckley)
My Days Are Numbered (Al Kooper)
Without Her (Harry Nilsson)
Just One Smile (Randy Newman)

SIDE TWO
I Can't Quit Her (Al Kooper)
Meagan's Gypsy Eyes (Steve Katz)
Somethin' Goin' On (Al Kooper)
House In The Country (Al Kooper)
The Modern Adventures Of Plato,
Diogenes & Freud (Al Kooper)
So Much Love/Underture
(Gerry Goffin/Carole King)

This debut album was extremely ambitious as a serious attempt at jazz/rock. At the time, it received more critical than commercial acclaim, probably because it became more and more jazz-oriented as it went on.

However, the tastefully chosen and carefully arranged cover versions were quite sufficient to make this an album of some note, and as well as making the UK chart for a single week, it spent over a year in the US chart without quite reaching the Top 40.

Although several tracks, such as 'Just One Smile', 'Without Her' and Al Kooper's 'I Can't Quit Her', could have been viable singles, no hits from the album ensued, and 1969 brought several personnel changes, including the departure of founder member Kooper.

Blood, Sweat & Tears was conceived by Kooper (keyboards, lead vocals) and Steve Katz (guitar, vocals), both of whom were ex-members of The Blues Project, a noted New York white R&B band. Jim Fielder (bass, ex-Buffalo Springfield) and drummer Bobby Colomby made up the project's rock quartet.

They were augmented by a horn section comprising New York jazzers cum session musicians Fred Lipsius (saxophone), trumpeters Randy Brecker and Jerry Weiss and Dick Halligan (trombone).

The band's second album, the inventively-titled Blood, Sweat & Tears, was hugely successful, selling two million copies in nine months. However, Child Is Father To The Man is a far more pioneering album, even down to its bizarrely intriguing sleeve.

A BREAK ON THE ORGAN

Al Kooper first achieved celebrity as the organ player on Bob Dylan's first big hit single, 1965's 'Like A Rolling Stone'. Kooper was a guitarist, but he infiltrated a Dylan recording session by arriving at the studio some time before the other musicians had arrived, in the hope that he could play with his hero.

Any idea he had of playing lead guitar disappeared when Dylan brought Mike Bloomfield into the studio, and Kooper thought he had lost any chance of being on a Dylan track, but as luck would have it, he noticed an empty seat behind the organ, and when 'Like A Rolling Stone' was being recorded, he hesitantly added organ fills. Listening to the completed track in the studio's control room, Dylan instructed producer Tom Wilson to increase the volume of the organ part, and even when Wilson protested that it had been played by someone who wasn't really an organ player, Dylan insisted that it should be louder. At the end of the day's recording, Dylan asked Kooper for his telephone number, which Kooper likened to Brigitte Bardot asking for the key to your hotel room.

BOOKENDS

SIMON & GARFUNKEL (1968)

Produced by Roy Halee
Total running time: 29.45

SIDE ONE
Bookends Theme (Paul Simon)
Save The Life Of My Child (Paul Simon)
America (Paul Simon)
Overs (Paul Simon)
Voices Of Old People
(Paul Simon & Art Garfunkel)
Old Friends (Paul Simon)

SIDE TWO
Bookends Theme (Paul Simon)
Fakin' It (Paul Simon)
Punky's Dilemma (Paul Simon)
Mrs. Robinson (Paul Simon)
A Hazy Shade Of Winter (Paul Simon)
At The Zoo (Paul Simon)

Released in the US by Columbia Records and
in the UK by CBS Records

fter their 1966 breakthrough with *Sounds Of Silence*, Paul Simon & Art Garfunkel had become major stars. Their late 1966 album, *Parsley, Sage, Rosemary & Thyme*, reached the US Top 5 and included their fourth US hit single in nine months, 'The Dangling Conversation'.

Bookends consolidated Simon's reputation as a deeply thoughtful songwriter, whose material could be taken to aesthetically desirable heights by the ethereal voice of Art Garfunkel.

The major project of 1967 for Simon was writing the music for 'The Graduate', a feature film starring Anne Bancroft as a mature housewife and introducing Dustin Hoffman as a young student whom she seduces.

Director Mike Nichols, who had enjoyed the *Parsley, Sage* LP, invited Simon to write original songs for the soundtrack of the movie, but felt that all but one of the new songs submitted by Simon were unsuitable.

Nichols thus began to use already existing Simon & Garfunkel songs in the film until Simon came up with new material. As a result, two of the rejected songs, 'Punky's Dilemma' and 'Overs', were available for the next Simon & Garfunkel album, *Bookends*.

The film brought considerable benefits to Simon & Garfunkel. The release of the soundtrack LP to 'The Graduate' topped the US chart for nine weeks, and gave *Bookends* a push start. The new album replaced 'The Graduate' at the top of the US album chart, staying there for seven weeks.

RHYMIN' SIMON

During the mid-'60s Paul Simon took time off from Simon & Garfunkel to collaborate with Bruce Woodley, a member of Australian folk quartet The Seekers, on a handful of songs of which two became hit singles.

Two of the songs they wrote together, 'I Wish You Could Be Here' and 'Red Rubber Ball', appeared on Come The Day, a 1966 LP by The Seekers which reached the Top 3 of the UK chart, while they also co-wrote 'Someday One Day', the quartet's fourth hit single which just failed to reach the UK Top 10.

Paul Simon also enjoyed extra-curricular activities as a producer – while living in the UK in 1965 he produced an album by legendary American singer/songwriter Jackson C. Frank, on which Al Stewart played guitar.

One of the best songs on Bookends, an album including many highlights, is 'America', one of several songs inspired by Simon's English girlfriend, Kathy, who is actually mentioned in the song by name. Kathy was also the inspiration behind other songs such as 'Homeward Bound' and (of course) 'Kathy's Song', and she was pictured on the album sleeve of Simon's first solo album, The Paul Simon Songbook, which had been released in 1965.

GREATEST HITS

STEVIE WONDER (1968)

Produced by * Henry Cosby, ** Clarence Paul, *** William Stevenson & Henry Cosby, **** Robert Gordy, ***** Dorsey Burnette, ****** Berry Gordy Jr., ******* Hal Davis & Marc Gordon, ******** Brian Holland & Lamont Dozier
Total running time: 43.12
Released in the US by Tamla Records and in the UK by Tamla-Motown Records

SIDE ONE
Shoo-Be-Doo-Be-Doo-Da-Day (Henry Cosby/Sylvia Moy/Stevie Wonder) *
**A Place In The Sun
(Ron Miller/Bryan Wells) ****
Uptight (Everything's Alright) (Henry Cosby/Stevie Wonder/Sylvia Moy) ***
Travelin' Man (Ron Miller/Bryan Wells) **
**High Heel Sneakers
(Robert Higgenbotham) *****
Sad Boy (Dorsey Burnette/Gerald Nelson) ****
Kiss Me Baby (Stevie Wonder/Clarence Paul) **
**Workout Stevie, Workout
(Clarence Paul/ Henry Cosby) ****

SIDE TWO
**Fingertips (Part 2)
(Henry Cosby/Clarence Paul) ******
**Hey Harmonica Man
(Marty Cooper/Lou Josie) *******
Contract On Love (Brian Holland/Lamont Dozier/Eddie Holland) ******
Castles In The Sand (Hal Davis/Frank Wilson/Marc Gordon/Mary O'Brien) ******
Nothing's Too Good For My Baby (William Stevenson/Henry Cosby/Sylvia Moy) ***
I Was Made To Love Her (Henry Cosby/Lula Hardaway/Sylvia Moy/Stevie Wonder) *
Blowin' In The Wind (Bob Dylan) **
I'm Wondering (Henry Cosby/Stevie Wonder/Sylvia Moy) *

Covering the period between mid-1963 and late 1967, this album demonstrates the then 17-year-old Stevie Wonder's growing maturity. The liveliest highlights are the raucous rave-up of 'Fingertips' and the similarly live 'High Heel Sneakers' and his early songwriting collaboration with Sylvia Moy and producer Hank Cosby on 'Uptight'.

Wonder's voice is more restrained, but in equally powerful form on his interpretation of Bob Dylan's classic protest song 'Blowin' In The Wind' (on which producer Cosby duets) and the soulful ballad, 'A Place In The Sun', which led to his first international smash hit, 'I Was Made To Love Her'. His mother, Lula Hardaway, receives a credit for that song, along with Cosby, Moy and Stevie himself as a songwriter.

The US version omits 'Shoo-Be-Doo-Be-Doo-Da-Day', 'Travelin' Man', 'High Heel Sneakers', 'Sad Boy' and 'Kiss Me Baby', but includes 'Hey Love' written by Clarence Paul & Morris Broadnax and produced by Clarence Paul.

The US version of this album included 12 of Wonder's first 13 US hit singles, seven of which ('Fingertips', 'Uptight', 'Nothing's Too Good', 'Blowin' In The Wind', 'A Place In The Sun', 'I Was Made To Love Her' and 'I'm Wondering') reached the US Top 20.

BOY WONDER

Stevie Wonder's debut single, 'I Call It Pretty Music (But The Old People Call It The Blues)', was released in August 1962, and included Marvin Gaye playing drums among the backing musicians. The end of that year saw the 12-year-old on a Motown package tour which also featured The Miracles, Marvin Gaye, Mary Wells and The Supremes.

Eight days after his 13th birthday in May 1963, a live concert in Detroit by Wonder was recorded for an album released with the slightly inaccurate title of Recorded Live – The 12 Year Old Genius, from which 'Fingertips' was excerpted as a two part single, and 'Fingertips Part 2' became the first ever live single to top the US chart.

When the live album also topped the US chart in late August 1963, Wonder became the first artist to simultaneously top the US singles, albums and R&B charts.

OGDEN'S NUT GONE FLAKE

THE SMALL FACES (1968)

Produced by Steve Marriott & Ronnie Lane
Total running time: 39.17
Released in the UK & US by Immediate Records

SIDE ONE
Ogden's Nut Gone Flake
(Marriott/Lane/McLagan/Jones)
Afterglow (Marriott/Lane)
Long Agos And Worlds Apart (McLagan)
Rene (Marriott/Lane)
Song Of A Baker (Marriott/Lane)
Lazy Sunday (Marriott/Lane)

SIDE TWO
Happiness Stan (Marriott/Lane)
Rollin' Over (Marriott/Lane)
The Hungry Intruder
(Marriott/Lane/McLagan)
The Journey (Marriott/Lane/McLagan/Jones)
Mad John (Marriott/Lane)
Happdaystoytown
(Marriott/Lane/McLagan/Jones)

T he Small Faces' finest line-up made its final appearance on this album, but it is perhaps best remembered because of its circular sleeve (to further extend its resemblance to a flattened tin of pipe tobacco). That made it, music apart, a far from user-friendly album, as it was prone to rolling off shelves.

Formed in London in 1965 when former child actor Steve Marriott (lead vocals, guitar) joined the trio of Ronnie Lane (bass, vocals), Kenny Jones (drums) and Jimmy Winston (keyboards), the group had their first UK Top 20 hit within six months, after which Winston left. He was replaced by Ian McLagan, who was not only in greater musical sympathy with his colleagues, but like them was short in stature (unlike the much taller Winston), making their group name,

chosen to reflect their 'mod' status, more appropriate – a 'face' was a leading 'mod' who set trends in fashion and outlook.

The Small Faces were instant 'mod' favourites, rivalling The Who in popularity in Swinging London.

Their second Top 10 single of 1968, 'Lazy Sunday', an easy-paced Kinks-like item sung by Marriott in a cockney accent, became their fourth Top 3 hit in just over two years. Soon afterwards, this album topped the UK chart for six weeks. Apart from the shape of the sleeve, the inclusion of between-tracks links by comedian Stanley Unwin was another gimmick, and although the cleverness of the gimmicks sometimes upstaged the music, this remains a daring and still enjoyable experimental album by a singles-oriented group.

NEW FACES

The group's dissolution came about when singer/guitarist Peter Frampton (pin-up front man of The Herd) guested with The Small Faces, establishing a rapport with Marriott, who decided they should form a new band and left The Small Faces in early 1969. Recruiting Greg Ridley on bass and drummer Jerry Shirley, they launched Humble Pie and their first 45, 'Natural Born Bugie', was a UK Top 5 hit.

His ex-colleagues had joined forces with vocalist Rod Stewart and guitarist Ron Wood (both ex-Jeff Beck Group) to form The Faces, a very popular live draw in the early '70s whose records were regularly outsold by Stewart's solo releases, and who split up in 1975 as a result. By then, Ronnie Lane had left to form his own band, Slim Chance, and Ron Wood had joined The Rolling Stones. In 1976, both 'Itchycoo Park' (one of the best-loved Small Faces hits) and 'Lazy Sunday' were reissued. Both made the UK chart and the group reformed, but with Ricky Wills (ex-Peter Frampton, ironically) replacing Lane, who preferred to continue with his solo career. After two disappointing albums, they disbanded.

WHEELS OF FIRE

CREAM (1968)

Produced by Felix Pappalardi
Total running time: 79.57
Released in the US by Atco Records and in the UK by Polydor Records

ream, formed in June 1966 by guitarist Eric Clapton (ex-John Mayall's Bluesbreakers), vocalist/bass player Jack Bruce (ex-Alexis Korner, Graham Bond Organization, Bluesbreakers and Manfred Mann) and drummer Ginger Baker, Bruce's colleague in the Korner and Bond bands, was the first of the so-called supergroups.

Their first and second LPs, *Fresh Cream* and *Disraeli Gears* (both released in 1967), were great successes, achieving gold status in the US and reaching the Top 10 of the UK album chart.

But *Wheels Of Fire*, a double LP containing one album of studio recordings and one of live tracks recorded at San Francisco's Fillmore Auditorium, turned out to be the trio's greatest achievement.

It topped the US album chart for a month and reached the UK Top 3, while 'White Room' was excerpted from the studio album to become a US Top 10/UK Top 30 single.

For many the highlight of *Wheels Of Fire* was the 16-minutes-plus live version of 'Spoonful', which became strongly associated with Cream.

The internal group politics as displayed here graphically illustrate why Cream fell apart three months after this album was released: the studio album includes four tracks from Bruce's songwriting partnership with poet/lyricist Pete Brown and three from the team of Baker and Mike Taylor, an avant garde jazz musician. Clapton is allowed two blues, Howlin' Wolf's 'Top Of The World' and Albert King's 'Bad Sign'.

At least the first side of the live LP gave him a chance to shine, with a brilliant 'Crossroads', which he had previously recorded as part of a studio group, Eric Clapton & The Powerhouse, and the mammoth 'Spoonful', leaving the second live side to a seven minute harmonica tour de force from Bruce and a 16-minute-plus Baker drum feature.

As the band that defined the supergroup genre, Cream personified both the advantages and pitfalls which could (and usually did) result.

The musical results were often spectacularly excellent and became both artistic and commercial successes. But the frequent antler-locking of giant egos made relationships fragile – it is hard to think of many supergroups which have continued to function uninterrupted for more than a couple of albums.

Bringing together several stars whose only common facet is their (often fading) fame can prove to be both frustrating and expensive (both commercially and artistically) – many supergroups only look good on paper, as has been proved far too often.

Maybe not such a bad idea for the lawyers and accountants who run the record industry, but more to do with profit than creativity…

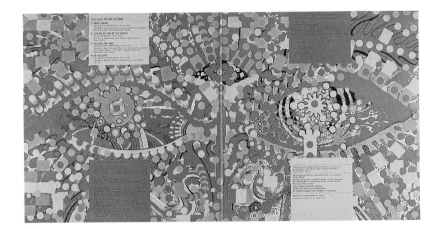

SIDE ONE
White Room *(Jack Bruce & Pete Brown)*
Sitting On Top Of The World *(Chester Burnett)*
Passing The Time *(Ginger Baker & Mike Taylor)*
As You Said *(Jack Bruce & Pete Brown)*

SIDE TWO
Pressed Rat And Warthog *(Ginger Baker & Mike Taylor)*
Politician *(Jack Bruce & Pete Brown)*
Those Were The Days *(Ginger Baker & Mike Taylor)*
Born Under A Bad Sign *(Booker T. Jones & William Bell)*
Deserted Cities Of The Heart *(Jack Bruce & Pete Brown)*

SIDE THREE
Crossroads *(Robert Johnson)*
Spoonful *(Willie Dixon)*

SIDE FOUR
Traintime *(Jack Bruce)*
Toad *(Ginger Baker)*

RUNNING CREAM

Cream's final gigs at London's Royal Albert Hall in November 1968 were filmed for television, and a posthumous album, Goodbye Cream, emerged in early 1969. This included 'Badge', a song co-written by Clapton and his friend, George Harrison of The Beatles, which became a UK Top 20 hit, on which Clapton sang lead and Harrison played rhythm guitar under the alias of 'L'Angelo Misterioso'. The album included live versions of 'Politician' and 'Sitting On Top Of The World' (both from the Wheels Of Fire studio LP) and a nine-minute-plus live version of the Skip James classic, 'I'm So Glad', with Clapton as lead vocalist as well as lead guitarist.

New Cream LPs continued to be released until 1972 – Best Of Cream, Live Cream, Live Cream Vol. 2 (all of which reached the Top 30 of the US chart) and Heavy Cream, by which time the individual members had all embarked on solo careers with varying degrees of success.

Clapton and Baker had worked together in the short-lived Blind Faith before Clapton formed Derek & The Dominos in 1970 and Baker launched his unwieldy 11-piece Airforce. After an acclaimed 1969 solo album, Songs For A Tailor, Bruce seemingly found it difficult to maintain that early success, and both he and Baker declined in commercial terms, while Clapton became a superstar. Despite Cream's short life span of around two and a half years, the group remains legendary.

TRUTH

JEFF BECK (1968)

SIDE ONE
Shapes Of Things
(P. Samwell-Smith/K. Relf/J. McCarty)
Let Me Love You *(J. Rod)*
Morning Dew *(B. Dobson/T. Rose)*
You Shook Me *(W. Dixon/J. B. Lenore)*
Ol' Man River *(J. Kern)*

SIDE TWO
Greensleeves *(Trad. arr A. Jeffrey)*
Rock My Plimsoul *(J. Rod)*
Beck's Bolero *(J. Page)*
Blues De Luxe *(J. Rod)*
I Ain't Superstitious *(W. Dixon)*

Produced by Mickie Most
Total running time: 40.14
*Released in the UK on EMI/Columbia and
in the US on Epic Records*

 eff Beck's guitar work on *Truth* was rarely bettered in the '60s, or in any other period. With Rod Stewart as vocalist, Ron Wood (nowadays a Rolling Stone) on bass and noted keyboard star Nicky Hopkins, guitar hero Beck was clearly on to a winner here.

After leaving The Yardbirds – he was on more hits than that band's other lead guitarists, Eric Clapton and Jimmy Page combined – he came in contact with the Midas touch of producer Mickie Most.

Most insisted on Beck himself (not by inclination a singer) being the vocalist on his debut single, 'Hi Ho Silver Lining', rather than Stewart, whom Most had allowed to sing on The Jeff Beck Group's debut album, widely regarded as Stewart's first major step to international superstardom, a status which Beck has yet to attain.

This result of their stormy union reached the US Top 20, but has never charted in Britain, though many still regard it as Beck's finest and most accessible work.

There are similarities between *Truth* and the first album by Led Zeppelin (formed by Beck's erstwhile Yardbirds colleague Page). Both albums included two songs written by legendary Chicago bluesman Willie Dixon, and both featured 'You Shook Me'.

The parallels didn't end there – on 'Beck's Bolero' (an instrumental written by Page) were Beck (lead), Page (rhythm), John Paul Jones (Page's Led Zep colleague, bass) and Keith Moon (credited as 'You Know Who', drums).

The composite songwriting credit name J. Rod, for three of the songs on *Truth*, is a songwriting pseudonym for Beck & Stewart, and among the album's many highlights are 'Morning Dew' (which was based on Tim Rose's acclaimed version), and the two Willie Dixon compositions, on which Beck's blues/rock guitar work is exceptional.

CHEAP THRILLS

BIG BROTHER & THE HOLDING COMPANY (1968)

SIDE ONE
Combination Of The Two (S. Andrew)
I Need A Man To Love (J. Joplin/S. Andrew)
Summertime (D. Heyward/G. Gershwin)
Piece Of My Heart (J. Ragovoy/B. Berns)

SIDE TWO
Turtle Blues (J. Joplin)
Oh, Sweet Mary (J. Joplin)
Ball And Chain (W. M. Thornton)

Produced by John Simon
Total running time: 37.14
Released in the US by Columbia Records and in the UK by CBS Records

Cheap Thrills was Big Brother & The Holding Company's crowning achievement, capturing the passion and pain in singer Janis Joplin's voice at its heartrending best.

It topped the US chart for eight weeks in 1968, but before the end of the year, the group disbanded when Joplin left for a solo career.

Big Brother & The Holding Company were well-regarded in San Francisco even before Texan vocalist Joplin joined them in mid-1966, but her arrival transformed them from worthy contenders into one of the biggest acts in the Bay Area. Formed in 1965 by Sam Andrew (vocals, lead guitar) and Peter Albin (bass, vocals), the group included James Gurley (guitar) and David Getz (drums).

When their manager invited Janis to return to California, where he had heard her singing in 1963, Joplin, whose marriage plans had just fallen through,

quickly accepted the offer, adding a new dimension to the group's psychedelic musical direction with her three octave vocal range.

Snapped up for management by Bob Dylan's erstwhile manager, Albert Grossman, the group then signed to Columbia Records for what was effectively their debut as a fully-realised act. But problems involved in capturing the group's magic in the studio led to producer John Simon including several live tracks on the album.

Simon received no producer credit on the sleeve, but nor did anyone else, although five engineers (including Joplin and Gurley) are named. The three standout tracks are the slow-burning version of 'Summertime', with Joplin's soulful wailing and an excellent guitar workout, her inspired version of Big Mama Thornton's 'Ball & Chain' and the sensational 'Piece Of My Heart', one of the quintessential Joplin performances.

FAR-OUT FRONTWOMAN

Janis Joplin's next recording project after Cheap Thrills (originally to be titled Sex, Drugs & Cheap Thrills) was I Got Dem Ol' Kozmic Blues Again Mama!, an album on which she fronted The Kozmic Blues Band, whose personnel changed with monotonous regularity. This first solo album was generally regarded as disappointing, its poor quality being attributed to Joplin's alcohol and drug habits.

Two months after the album's late 1969 release, the band fell apart. Almost simultaneously, after a year of suspended animation, Big Brother & The Holding Company resurfaced with a new line-up of Andrew, Getz, Albin, guitarist David Schallock and vocalist Nick Gravenites. When Joplin joined them onstage in April 1970, rumours of a reunion circulated. Instead, she recruited The Full Tilt Boogie Band, who played on her finest original LP. Titled Pearl (Joplin's nickname for herself), it topped the US chart for nine weeks in 1971, and included her magnificent version of Kris Kristofferson's 'Me & Bobby McGee'. Tragically, Joplin died of a drug overdose on 4 October 1970, just prior to completing the album.

SWEETHEART OF THE RODEO

THE BYRDS (1968)

SIDE ONE
You Ain't Goin' Nowhere (B. Dylan)
I Am A Pilgrim (Arranged by Roger McGuinn/Chris Hillman)
The Christian Life (I. Louvin/C. Louvin)
You Don't Miss Your Water (W. Bell)
You're Still On My Mind (I. McDaniel)
Pretty Boy Floyd (W. Guthrie)

SIDE TWO
Hickory Wind (G. Parsons/B. Buchanan)
One Hundred Years From Now (G. Parsons)
Blue Canadian Rockies (C. Walker)
Life In Prison (M. Haggard/G. Sanders)
Nothing Was Delivered (B. Dylan)

Produced by Gary Usher
Total running time: 32.11

Released in the US by Columbia Records and in the UK by CBS Records

weetheart Of The Rodeo is the most influential Byrds LP – the first commercially successful album to fuse country music with rock.

The new blood needed to revive the group's fortunes (temporarily arrested by their million-selling *Greatest Hits* album in late 1967) came in the shape of Chris Hillman's cousin, drummer Kevin Kelley, ex-The Rising Sons, a seminal Los Angeles group which included Ry Cooder and Taj Mahal.

More crucial was Roger McGuinn's hiring of Gram Parsons as vocalist and keyboard player, without realising (or so he claimed) that Parsons was only interested in exposing country music to a rock audience.

This crusade, which later made Parsons legendary, first became apparent earlier in 1968 with *Safe At Home*, made by Parsons as leader of The International Submarine Band and acknowledged as the first ever country/rock album, but when it flopped, Parsons needed a new vehicle to pursue his dream. Joining The Byrds was a huge stroke of luck.

The album's sleeve (a pre-war illustration with drawings of spurs and cowboy wear) emphasised the new direction, while some of the music was vintage country, like the traditional 'I Am A Pilgrim', followed by an equally religious Louvin Brothers song.

Bob Dylan's 'You Ain't Goin' Nowhere' was a minor hit, and Parsons was the only group member who contributed songs to this historic album.

SQUAWK ROCK

The group's first album of 1968, The Notorious Byrd Brothers, was largely the work of Roger McGuinn (who had changed his first name from Jim due to his interest in the Subud spiritual faith) and Chris Hillman, as their three original colleagues (Gene Clark, David Crosby & Michael Clarke) had either left the group or were on the point of doing so.

Since Clark had been absent for some time, Parsons joined as Crosby's replacement, and even though their musical approaches differed, the two were the most disruptive influences of the group's 10 year existence. Parsons left the group soon after the album was released, refusing to embark on a South African tour (ostensibly due to his objection to apartheid, but according to other sources, because he wanted to hang out with a new friend, Rolling Stone Keith Richard).

With no replacement available, tour manager Carlos Bernal was forced to deputise. Parsons with pedal steel guitarist Sneaky Pete Kleinow, who played on Sweetheart, and Hillman, who left The Byrds after the South African tour, then formed The Flying Burrito Brothers, leaving McGuinn in sole command of The Byrds. Ironically, in view of the problems the group had experienced from the move into country music, he decided to continue in that vein.

WAITING FOR THE SUN

THE DOORS (1968)

SIDE ONE
Hello, I Love You (The Doors)
Love Street (The Doors)
Not To Touch The Earth (The Doors)
Summer's Almost Gone (The Doors)
Wintertime Love (The Doors)
The Unknown Soldier (The Doors)

SIDE TWO
Spanish Caravan (The Doors)
My Wild Love (The Doors)
We Could Be So Good Together (The Doors)
Yes, The River Knows (The Doors)
Five To One (The Doors)

Produced by Paul A.Rothchild
Total running time: 33.14
Released in the US & UK by Elektra Records

This was the first album by The Doors to top the US chart and also their first to reach the UK chart. It finds Jim Morrison at his didactic best. After the colossal success of their eponymous debut LP in 1967, and the slightly smaller achievement of the same year's follow-up, *Strange Days*, which merely went gold rather than platinum, the group had released two significant singles, 'The Unknown Soldier', an anti-war song, and a second million-selling Number 1 single, 'Hello, I Love You'.

'The Unknown Soldier' was notable because the group assembled a short promotional film in which vocalist Morrison was apparently shot by a firing squad – banned by most TV stations in the US, it received considerable publicity as a result. Morrison had studied film-making at UCLA, where he first met

Doors keyboard player Ray Manzarek, who was on the same course.

While the short film did not deserve awards, it was one of the earliest clips made for a single, which gives it some retrospective historical value.

Reviewers likened 'Hello, I Love You' to 'All Day And All Of The Night' by The Kinks, and its riff-based construction was indeed along similar lines.

Of the other tracks, most attention was paid to 'Spanish Caravan', with its Segovia-like beginning by Robbie Krieger on Spanish guitar, followed by a heavy repeated electric riff before Morrison's ethereal vocal. This track is noteworthy for its use of two guest bass players, jazzman Leroy Vinegar on acoustic bass and Doug Lubahn, of Elektra label-mates Clear Light, on electric. The Doors, idiosyncratically, never included a dedicated bass player.

THE LIZARD KING

The sleeve of the Waiting For The Sun *LP featured the words of a poem by Jim Morrison, 'The Celebration Of The Lizard', which seemed to have little to do with the songs on the album, although this 'song' later appeared on the group's 1970 double album,* Absolutely Live. *Similarly, there was no song titled 'Waiting For The Sun' on this album, but such a song did appear on the fifth Doors studio album,* Morrison Hotel. *In between came their most experimental album, 1969's* The Soft Parade, *which climaxed with the eight minute plus title track, and included more US hit singles than any other Doors LP.*

As the first Doors LP with individual songwriting credits, The Soft Parade *suggested that Ray Manzarek (who had incidentally played the bass parts on early records using foot pedals on his organ) had played a lesser part in writing the group's hits than many had presumed, although it was less of a surprise to find drummer John Densmore's name absent from the songwriting credits. While it sold enough to go gold like its three predecessors, it was the group's first album which peaked outside the Top 3 of the US chart.*

HOLLIES' GREATEST

THE HOLLIES (1968)

Produced by Ron Richards
Total Running Time: 39.16
Released in the UK on EMI/Parlophone Records

SIDE ONE
I Can't Let Go (Taylor/Gorgoni)
Bus Stop (Gouldman)
We're Through (Ransford)
Carrie Anne (Clarke/Hicks/Nash)
Here I Go Again (Shuman/Westlake)
King Midas In Reverse
(Clarke/Hicks/Nash)
Yes I Will (Goffin/Titelman)

SIDE TWO
I'm Alive (Ballard Jnr.)
Just One Look (Payne/Carroll)
On A Carousel (Clarke/Hicks/Nash)
Stay (Williams)
Look Through Any Window
(Gouldman/Silverman)
Stop Stop Stop (Clarke/Hicks/Nash)
Jennifer Eccles (Clarke/Nash)

This Manchester beat group proved to be remarkably consistent as UK hit-makers – 13 of the 14 tracks on this UK Number 1 album were Top 10 hits inside five years.

Formed in the early '60s around the vocal harmonies of Allan Clarke and Graham Nash (previously The Two Teens, an Everly Brothers-styled duo), the group's nucleus included guitarist Tony Hicks and drummer Bobby Elliott.

Early success came with cover versions of American hits like 'Stay' by Maurice Williams & The Zodiacs and Doris Troy's 'Just One Look'. But Clarke, Nash & Hicks became a notable writing team, first under the joint *nom-de-plume* of L. Ransford. Their first hit composition was 1964's 'We're Through', while eight of the 12 tracks on the 1967 Everly Brothers album, *Two Yanks In England*, were by Ransford. They went on to use their own names on the credits.

From 1965's 'Yes I Will' (their first UK Number 1) to mid-1966's 'Bus Stop' (one of two hits from fellow Mancunian Graham Gouldman, later a founder member of 10cc), the hits were covers, but from then until mid-1968 (when this album was released), all songs were group originals.

The formula ended when 'King Midas In Reverse' peaked outside the Top 10. Conceived by Nash, that single was released against the advice of producer Ron Richards, and in late 1968 Nash, who had objected to the planned *Hollies Sing Dylan* album, left the group to join the ex-Byrd David Crosby and Stephen Stills (ex-Buffalo Springfield) in Crosby, Stills & Nash.

Hollies' Greatest was not released in the US, the nearest equivalents being the *Greatest Hits* albums that were released on Imperial (1967) and Epic (1973). During the '70s, The Hollies underwent numerous personnel changes. Clarke left the band twice during the decade for largely unsuccessful attempts at solo stardom. Only Hicks and Elliott remained ever-present.

TIMELESS CLASSICS

The Hollies recorded their second Number 1 single in 1969, 'He Ain't Heavy, He's My Brother'. But it took nearly two decades for it to reach the top place in the charts. The song was a success on its original release in late 1969, when it reached Number 3 in the UK and sold more than a million copies worldwide. But it was when it was used in a 1988 TV commercial for Miller Lite beer, and was reissued as a single that, nearly 20 years after its original 1969 release, it became the group's second UK Number 1.

It was also their first Top 10 hit since 'The Air That I Breathe' had achieved that status in the US and UK in early 1974.

SUPER SESSION

MIKE BLOOMFIELD, AL KOOPER, STEVE STILLS (1968)

SIDE ONE
Albert's Shuffle (M. Bloomfield/A. Kooper)
Stop (J. Ragavoy/M. Shuman)
Man's Temptation (C. Mayfield)
His Holy Modal Majesty
(A. Kooper/M. Bloomfield)
Really (M. Bloomfield/A. Kooper)

SIDE TWO
It Takes A Lot To Laugh, It Takes A Train To
Cry (B. Dylan)
Season Of The Witch (D. Leitch)
You Don't Love Me (W. Cobb)
Harvey's Tune (H. Brooks).

Produced by Al Kooper
Total running time: 50.36
Released in the US by Columbia Records and in the UK by CBS Records

The magic in this gold album comes from it being unplanned. Vocalist/keyboard player Al Kooper, a founder member of Blood, Sweat & Tears, had left that band after one album, taking a job as A&R man/producer with Columbia Records.

In the absence of any acts he wanted to sign or produce, he organised a studio jam session with other known musicians, hoping that the results might provide inspiration.

Guitarist Mike Bloomfield had made his name with the Paul Butterfield Blues Band and knew Kooper as they had played together on Bob Dylan's 'Like A Rolling Stone', and when he agreed to participate, it was decided that he and Kooper should each select another participant. Kooper chose his old friend, bass player Harvey Brooks; Bloomfield chose drummer 'Fast' Eddie Hoh, who had worked with The Mamas & Papas.

The first side of the album, which included three tunes written on the spot, was recorded in nine hours.

When Kooper woke up the next morning, Bloomfield had left a note saying that he had gone home, as he had been unable to sleep due to an ingrowing toenail. With the studio booked, Kooper had to quickly find another guitarist, and luckily called Stephen Stills. He was at a loose end as Buffalo Springfield had just broken up.

Stills played on the second side of the album, a highlight of which is the eleven minute plus version of Donovan's 'Season Of The Witch', featuring his classic wah-wah guitar solo.

LIVE WIRE

Al Kooper's first major hit came when he was 20 years old, as one of the songwriters of the million-selling Gary Lewis & The Playboys hit, 'This Diamond Ring', in 1965. After that, he was a founder member of The Blues Project, a New York R&B group which gained a strong live reputation, but never became internationally famous.

He and guitarist Steve Katz left the group to form Blood, Sweat & Tears, the first ever jazz/rock group. However, internal power struggles threatened to destroy the group until Kooper left after their first album, whereupon BS&T became extremely successful. Kooper's next project was Super Session, and after its somewhat unexpected success, he decided to recreate it, although this time live in front of an audience at the Fillmore West in San Francisco.

Bloomfield was there on the first two nights of the scheduled three night stand but he was absent for the third, having checked into hospital suffering from insomnia. Kooper began calling local guitarists, and Elvin Bishop, Steve Miller and Carlos Santana agreed to turn out.

Miller's work could not be used for contractual reasons, but Bishop appeared on the eventual live double album, The Live Adventures Of Mike Bloomfield & Al Kooper, as did Santana, who had never previously appeared on an album.

ASTRAL WEEKS

VAN MORRISON (1968)

SIDE ONE
In The Beginning
Astral Weeks (Morrison)
Beside You (Morrison)
Sweet Thing (Morrison)
Cypress Avenue (Morrison)

SIDE TWO
Afterwards
The Way Young Lovers Do (Morrison)
Madame George (Morrison)
Ballerina (Morrison)
Slim Slow Slider (Morrison)

Produced by Lewis Merenste
Total running time: 47.16

Released in the US and UK on Warner Bros Records

Having moved to the US after the disintegration of Them, Van Morrison had made a good start to his solo career on New York producer Bert Berns' Bang label. His first solo single, 'Brown Eyed Girl', made the US Top 10 in 1967.

However, the ever-restless Morrison was displeased when Bang released an album of what he considered largely unfinished tracks, and when Berns died unexpectedly at the end of that year, Morrison looked for a new record deal. Warner Bros president, Joe Smith, signed him in early 1968, after which Morrison recorded this masterpiece, considered by critics to be one of the outstanding albums of all time. Largely unencumbered by expectations, he spent two days in the studio with a group of jazz musicians.

The line-up included guitarist Jay Berliner, Richard Davis on double bass and Modern Jazz Quartet drummer Connie Kay, plus horn player John Payne and a vibraphone player. Morrison emerged with a fine album.

Johnny Rivers, the American folk/rock star, had a US hit in 1970 with his version of Morrison's 'Into The Mystic' but few of these songs have become hits, either for Van or anyone else. It is unrewarding to analyse the lyrics – Morrison has neither confirmed nor denied suggestions made by others (apart from his strange claim that a line in 'Madame George' which had been interpreted as referring to a drag queen was actually about being bored by a game of dominoes!). He once told a journalist that he thought it was about a piece of Swiss cheese...

SLOW SUCCESS

When it was released in the US in 1968, Astral Weeks did not reach the Billboard album chart, and has actually never done so. Nor has it ever been listed in the UK album chart – it was not released in the UK until 1969, after several hundred expensive US import copies had been sold in British record shops. It did not achieve gold status (500,000 sales) until over ten years after its initial release.

Van Morrison's next album, Moondance (his first of the '70s), seemed much more direct, eventually attaining platinum status and including a US Top 40 hit single and any number of songs which others have successfully covered. One explanation for the unceasing acclaim which has accrued to Astral Weeks is that it was one of the favourites of the 'in crowd' of the period; Jimi Hendrix supposedly watched several concerts by Morrison open-mouthed, and members of superhip bands like Quicksilver Messenger Service and Big Brother & The Holding Company were also seen at his mystical live shows. Perhaps Morrison's greatest achievement with this album was to produce a work so obviously brilliant that it could not be criticised, yet its lyrics defied all attempts at analysis and explanation. As a rock critic remarked, 'You can't say why it's so great, it just is.'

ELECTRIC LADYLAND

JIMI HENDRIX EXPERIENCE (1968)

Produced by Jimi Hendrix
Total running time: 75.28
Released in the UK by Track Records and in the US by Reprise Records

SIDE ONE
And The Gods Made Love (Hendrix)
Electric Ladyland (Hendrix)
Crosstown Traffic (Hendrix)
Voodoo Chile (Hendrix)

SIDE TWO
Little Miss Strange (Redding)
Long Hot Summer Night (Hendrix)
Come On (Earl King)
Gipsy Eyes (Hendrix)
Burning Of The Midnight Lamp (Hendrix)

SIDE THREE
Rainy Day, Dream Away (Hendrix)
1983 (A Merman I Should Turn To Be) (Hendrix)
Moon, Turn The Tides... Gently Gently Away (Hendrix)

SIDE FOUR
Still Raining Still Dreaming (Hendrix)
House Burning Down (Hendrix)
All Along The Watchtower (Dylan)
Voodoo Chile (slight return)

Electric Ladyland was the culmination of Hendrix's progress into new musical areas. Although he completed another two albums before his death, both seemed unnecessarily lacking in quality control.

The recording sessions for this album were spread over several months, as The Experience were also fulfilling concert bookings at the same time, which produced a somewhat diverse feel, from the half-speed backwards vocal of 'And The Gods Made Love' to the long bluesy version of 'Voodoo Chile' with Steve Winwood playing organ and Jefferson Airplane's Jack Casady on bass.

Other guests on the album included Al Kooper (piano on 'Long Hot Summer Night'), drummer Buddy Miles on 'Rainy Day, Dream Away' and 'Still Raining Still Dreaming', and Chris Wood of Traffic (flute on '1983').

Electric Ladyland was the only Hendrix release to top the US chart. It included four hit singles: 'Burning Of The Midnight Lamp' was the group's fourth and last UK hit of 1967, 'All Along The Watchtower' (from Bob Dylan's John Wesley Harding) was a UK Top 5 hit and the only Hendrix single to reach the US Top 20.

'Crosstown Traffic' was the last US hit by the Experience (his last two US hit singles were credited to Hendrix alone), and 'Voodoo Chile', released in Britain two months after Hendrix's untimely death in September 1970, was his only UK Number 1 single.

A LOOSE CANNON

The third and last album by The Experience (consisting of bassist Noel Redding and drummer Mitch Mitchell) caused controversy due to its eye-catching sleeve. Hendrix didn't like it – it was done in a hurry without his knowledge. The sleeve he had commissioned, which was used for the US version of the album, was not ready when Track needed it.

Hendrix was one of rock music's pioneers, although his tendency towards self-indulgence came to the fore when Chas Chandler, who had brought Hendrix to Europe and was his manager, ceased managing him around the time of this album's release in late 1968. Soon afterwards, Hendrix fell out with Redding and, in mid-1969, Mitchell.

Hendrix commissioned the construction of a recording studio in New York, naming it 'Electric Lady' after this album, but sadly only used it on a handful of occasions – soon after his appearance at the 1970 Isle Of Wight festival, he died in London.

The cause of death, according to a pathologist's report, was 'inhalation of vomit due to barbiturate intoxication' – a hugely unnecessary waste of an Olympian talent.

THE VILLAGE GREEN PRESERVATION SOCIETY

THE KINKS (1968)

SIDE ONE
The Village Green Preservation Society
(R. D. Davies)
Do You Remember Walter (R. D. Davies)
Picture Book (R. D. Davies)
Johnny Thunder (R. D. Davies)
The Last Of The Steam-Powered Trains
(R. D. Davies)
Big Sky (R. D. Davies)
Sitting By The Riverside (R. D. Davies)

SIDE TWO
Animal Farm (R. D. Davies)
Village Green (R. D. Davies)
Starstruck (R. D. Davies)
Phenomenal Cat (R. D. Davies)
All Of My Friends Were There
(R. D. Davies)
Wicked Annabella (R. D. Davies)
Monica (R. D. Davies)
People Take Pictures Of Each Other
(R. D. Davies)

Produced by Ray Davies
Total running time: 40.07
Released in the UK by Pye Records and in the US by Reprise Records

his LP sold poorly, but, in retrospect, this can be seen as due more to public inability to recognise its pioneering qualities – it is widely regarded as the very first concept album – than to any artistic shortcomings.

Leader/lead vocalist Ray Davies, one of the most original and talented songwriters in the world, was nostalgic for old values and traditions, and this album was designed to illustrate the point that constant progress is not necessarily the advantage it may seem.

The title track is a litany of things that Davies felt might be in danger of extinction, and is curiously similar to today's 'green' philosophy of the need to preserve rather than destroy the quainter and most lovable elements of the past – unfortunately, some of the things Davies listed have more or less vanished ('little shops, china cups and virginity'), but the message of the song is as relevant today as it was found irrelevant in the '60s.

As well as failing to reach the UK or US charts, the album was released (in 12-track form) and quickly withdrawn before being reissued a few weeks later, with two tracks ('Days', a hit single two months before, and 'Mr. Songbird') omitted, and five new tracks added. The Who's Pete Townshend credited it as a major inspiration for his rock operas.

SINGING COMMENTATORS

North London quartet The Kinks were formed by brothers Ray and Dave Davies, who both sang and played guitar, although Ray's strength was as a vocalist and songwriter and his younger brother was a more talented lead guitarist. Dave Davies was in R&B group The Ravens, which also included bass player Pete Quaife and, briefly, Ray Davies, whose songs attracted the attention of impresario (and ex-pop star) Larry Page. Page's interest in demos made by the Davies brothers, Quaife and drummer Mick Avory led to the group, who Page named The Kinks, signing with Pye Records.

Their third single, 'You Really Got Me', with its heavy guitar riff, topped the UK singles chart and reached the US Top 10 in 1964. The carbon-copy follow-up, 'All Day And All Of The Night', was a UK Top 3/US Top 10 hit at the end of the year, and 'Tired Of Waiting For You' was their second UK Number 1/third US Top 10 hit in 1965. Thereafter, the group's US hits were mainly minor – UK Top 10 classics such as 'Dedicated Follower Of Fashion' and 'Waterloo Sunset' were far less popular there. By then, Ray Davies's songwriting had evolved from the neo-heavy metal of the early hits to witty and thought-provoking comments on current trends and on the vanishing world in which he grew up.

THE BEATLES

THE BEATLES (1968)

Produced by George Martin
Total running time: 93.40
Released in the UK by Parlophone Records
and in the US by Capitol Records

SIDE ONE
Back In The USSR (Lennon/McCartney)
Dear Prudence (Lennon/McCartney)
Glass Onion (Lennon/McCartney)
Ob-La-Di, Ob-La-Da (Lennon/McCartney)
Wild Honey Pie (Lennon/McCartney)
The Continuing Story Of Bungalow Bill
(Lennon/McCartney)
While My Guitar Gently Weeps (Harrison)
Happiness Is A Warm Gun
(Lennon/McCartney)

SIDE TWO
Martha My Dear (Lennon/McCartney)
I'm So Tired (Lennon/McCartney)
Blackbird (Lennon/McCartney)
Piggies (Harrison)
Rocky Raccoon (Lennon/McCartney)
Don't Pass Me By (Starkey)
Why Don't We Do It In The Road
(Lennon/McCartney)
I Will (Lennon/McCartney)
Julia (Lennon/McCartney)

SIDE THREE
Birthday (Lennon/McCartney)
Yer Blues (Lennon/McCartney)
Mother Nature's Son (Lennon/McCartney)
Everybody's Got Something To Hide Except
Me And My Monkey (Lennon/McCartney)
Sexy Sadie (Lennon/McCartney)
Helter Skelter (Lennon/McCartney)
Long, Long, Long (Harrison)

SIDE FOUR
Revolution 1 (Lennon/McCartney)
Honey Pie (Lennon/McCartney)
Savoy Truffle (Harrison)
Cry Baby Cry (Lennon/McCartney)
Revolution 9 (Lennon/McCartney)
Good Night (Lennon/McCartney)

By this time in The Beatles' career, the prolific and solid gold songwriting partnership between John Lennon & Paul McCartney had begun to tarnish.

Although all the tracks they wrote separately are jointly credited (as they always were during the group's active life), many of the Lennon/McCartney songs here were written by one or the other. Which is not to suggest that this is a 30 track washout — far from it.

McCartney's brilliant parody/pastiche of The Beach Boys, 'Back In The USSR', is a very strong start, and Lennon's wistful 'Dear Prudence' is most acceptable.

'Wild Honey Pie' lasts less than a minute and seems to be a whimsical acoustic rehearsal by McCartney alone for the equally whimsical music-hall styled 'Honey Pie'. Harrison's 'While My Guitar Gently Weeps' is another highlight, although Lennon's 'Warm Gun' perfectly demonstrates his need for lyrical restraint.

'Revolution 1', the slower version of 'Revolution' (the B-side of the 'Hey Jude' single) is fine, but the similarly titled 'Revolution 9', is very different, an unlistenable eight minutes plus sound collage of tape loops with occasional shouts of 'Number 9'. Complete rubbish.

This would certainly have been a great single LP, but as a double, it was sometimes self-indulgent, although the good tracks outnumber the others. The Beatles deserved praise, however, for undertaking such a radical project.

APPLE PRESSING

The plain white laminated sleeve was embossed with the words 'The BEATLES' and initial UK pressings of the double album were consecutively numbered, supposedly to convey the impression that it was a limited edition, which it patently wasn't — sales by the end of 1970 had exceeded six million copies.

During the recording of the album (which took five months from start to finish), Ringo Starr left the band, but was persuaded to return before the news was widely known. During the same five months, the group also launched their own record label, Apple, on which all their own future recordings and those of acts they signed to the label would appear.

SAILOR

STEVE MILLER BAND (1968)

SIDE ONE
Song For Our Ancestors (Steve Miller)
Dear Mary (Steve Miller)
My Friend (T. Davis/B. Scaggs)
Living In The USA (Steve Miller)

SIDE TWO
Quicksilver Girl (Steve Miller)
Lucky Man (Jimmy Peterman)
Gangster Of Love (John Watson)
You're So Fine (Jimmy Reed)
Overdrive (Boz Scaggs)
Dime-A-Dance Romance (Boz Scaggs)

Produced by The Steve Miller Band & Glyn Johns
Total running time: 34.31
Released in the US & UK by Capitol

Steve Miller had exhausted Chicago's possibilities as far as the blues circuit was concerned, when he heard of the growing psychedelic San Francisco scene. He moved there in late 1966, signing with Capitol Records in 1967.

His band's debut album, *Children Of The Future*, was a moderate success, but working again with British producer/engineer Glyn Johns, this, their second LP of 1968, was a masterpiece.

It featured extraordinary sound effects like the introductory fog horns on the spacey instrumental, 'Song For Our Ancestors', which were recorded under San Francisco's Golden Gate Bridge by Miller and Johns as boats passed by. The track ends with the sound of falling rain which continues into the stately 'Dear Mary' – another high point.

After the more urgent 'My Friend' with its feedback guitar comes 'Living In The USA', Miller's first (minor) US hit single, with dragstrip sound effects.

Side Two starts with the beautiful 'Quicksilver Girl', and includes more evidence of Miller's blues orientation, with covers of Johnny 'Guitar' Watson's 'Gangster Of Love' (thereafter associated as much with Miller as with Watson) and the Jimmy Reed song, as well as the exquisite country blues guitar intro to 'Lucky Man'.

Singer/guitarist Boz Scaggs's 'Overdrive' was also outstanding, although soon after this album was released, he and keyboard player Jim Peterman decided to quit the band.

That left a trio of Miller (vocals, guitar), Lonnie Turner (bass) and Tim Davis (drums, vocals).

Sailor became Miller's first album to reach the US Top 30, but has undeservedly never reached the UK album chart.

FRIEND TO TWO TOP PAULS

Steve Miller was shown his first guitar chords by Mary Ford, the wife of the great Les Paul, who were friends of Miller's parents. Paul, the legendary guitarist who broke his right arm and then chose to have it re-set in a position that would enable him to continue to play the guitar, remained a good friend and a considerable influence on Miller.

The Miller Band's next (third) LP, Brave New World, featured an unlikely guest star in the shape of one Paul Ramon (better known as Paul McCartney). Miller was at Abbey Road studios in London mixing some tracks for the new album with Johns while The Beatles were also recording at Abbey Road with Johns as engineer, and Miller found himself jamming with McCartney.

The result was 'My Dark Hour' – when Miller asked his famous collaborator what should be done about the songwriting and musician's credits on the track, McCartney told him to use the name Paul Ramon, a pseudonym he had briefly utilised at an early point in his career with The Beatles.

WHO KNOWS WHERE THE TIME GOES

JUDY COLLINS (1968)

SIDE ONE
Hello, Hooray (Rolf Kempf)
Story Of Isaac (Leonard Cohen)
My Father (Judy Collins)
Someday Soon (Ian Tyson)
Who Knows Where The Time Goes
(Sandy Denny)

SIDE TWO
Poor Immigrant (Bob Dylan)
First Boy I Loved (Robin Williamson)
Bird On The Wire (Leonard Cohen)
Pretty Polly
(Trad. arr. Judy Collins & Michael Sahl)

Produced by David Anderle
Total running time: 41.02
Released in the US & UK by Elektra Records

The possessor of an incredibly pure voice which made her famous on the world's folk circuit, Judy Collins was a brilliant interpreter of others' songs more often than a prolific songwriter, as this timeless album demonstrates.

For *Who Knows Where The Time Goes*, Collins' new and more rock-oriented producer, David Anderle, had introduced Collins to Stephen Stills, who had then only recently left Buffalo Springfield and was in the midst of planning a new group with David Crosby and Graham Nash.

Stills contributes guitar or bass on most of this album, which features a stellar rhythm section of Chris Ethridge (a founder member of The Flying Burrito Brothers) on bass and Jim Gordon (later a member of Derek & The Dominos with Eric Clapton) on drums, along with pianist Michael Sahl.

Several other interesting musicians also appear. These include the lead guitarist James Burton (who enjoys the rare distinction of having worked alongside both of the Elvises, Presley and Costello), pedal steel virtuoso Buddy Emmons and the eccentric genius Van Dyke Parks on piano.

As well as the usual dose of Leonard Cohen material – 'Bird On The Wire' is spectacular here – and the obligatory Bob Dylan classic, the two most outstanding tracks are 'Someday Soon', the story of a rodeo rider by Canadian singer/songwriter Ian Tyson (which he had recorded with his then wife as Ian & Sylvia), and 'Who Knows Where The Time Goes', a beautiful song written by Sandy Denny of Fairport Convention.

MARINE LIFE

While this album was being recorded, and for around a year thereafter, Judy Collins and Stephen Stills were involved romantically as well as musically. The first song on the first Crosby, Stills & Nash LP is the gentle epic 'Suite: Judy Blue Eyes', which was inspired by (and sung to) Judy Collins.

She did not pursue the musical direction of this album, opting for a quite different approach on *Whales & Nightingales*, her next LP, which included 'Farewell To Tarwathie', a track on which the singer was backed by the eerie sound of humpback whales.

'Rolling Stone' writer P.J. O'Rourke described a trip he made on the Amazon river during which he claimed that it was proved to him that dolphins enjoyed the music of Judy Collins. When a New York book editor sang 'Who Knows Where The Time Goes', after which the rest of the party joined in on 'Someday Soon' and 'Suzanne' (the Leonard Cohen song from her In My Life album), there was considerable dolphin activity.

Such activity was absent during the assembled entourage's impromptu performances of 'Smoke Gets In Your Eyes' and 'Can't Help Falling In Love', but returned strongly during the assembled company's rendition of 'Both Sides Now' from the Collins' *Wildflowers* album.

BEGGARS BANQUET

THE ROLLING STONES (1968)

Produced by Jimmy Miller
Total running time: 41.22
Released in the UK by Decca Records and
in the US by London Records

SIDE ONE
Sympathy For The Devil (Jagger/Richard)
No Expectations (Jagger/Richard)
Dear Doctor (Jagger/Richard)
Parachute Woman (Jagger/Richard)
Jig-Saw Puzzle (Jagger/Richard)

SIDE TWO
Street Fighting Man (Jagger/Richard)
Prodigal Son (Rev. Robert Wilkins)
Stary Cat Blues (Jagger/Richard)
Factory Girl (Jagger/Richard)
Salt Of The Earth (Jagger/Richard)

Beggars Banquet was both one of the finest albums of the late '60s and another instalment in the by then familiar dispute between The Rolling Stones and Decca. The argument this time was over the sleeve – the group favoured a photograph of a toilet wall with the album credits mingled with irrelevant scribbling of the type found in many public conveniences.

Decca turned down the proposed sleeve design, despite Mick Jagger's protestations that he found the sleeve of an album by fellow Decca artist Tom Jones offensive, as it portrayed a nuclear explosion. The inevitable compromise was a stark invitation card to a function. The inside of the gatefold featured a Gothic sepia-tinted photograph of the quintet apparently sated with food and alcohol and a hint of black magic.

The significant opening track, concerning the struggle between black and white (magic) which Jagger appeared to sing from the point of view of the devil, was particularly celebrated for its line about the protagonist being present when the Kennedys (John and Robert) were killed.

Similarly well-known was 'Street Fighting Man', which was banned by several US radio stations on the grounds that it might incite unrest. These two tracks were obvious stand-outs, but several others, including 'Stray Cat Blues', the saga of a jailbait groupie, and 'No Expectations', were equally impressive.

POOR BEGGAR

Beggars Banquet was the final original Rolling Stones album in which Brian Jones was involved, although it is generally agreed that his musical contributions here were at best negligible.

Jones had become trapped in a downward spiral of drug abuse largely caused by the realisation that despite having been a founder member, his position within the group was under threat, as they had never recorded any of his songs – early corporate songwriting credits to Nanker/Phelge had long since ended in favour of the more accurate Jagger/Richard.

By 1968, Jones was rarely allowed to play anything significant in the recording studio due to his increasing unreliability. He had been arrested and found guilty of possession of drugs on several occasions in 1967/68, and had narrowly escaped imprisonment, but then so had Mick Jagger and Keith Richards, who had been respectively sentenced to three months and a year in prison on drug charges, until they were the subject of an editorial headed 'Who breaks a butterfly on a wheel?' by William Rees-Mogg, editor of The Times, protesting about the imposition of prison sentences for such minor peccadillos.

Ultimately, it came down to Jones having no allies within the group, which by this time was controlled by Jagger and Richard, particularly after original manager Andrew Oldham's replacement by New York entrepreneur Allen Klein.

EDIZIONE D'ORO

FOUR SEASONS (1969)

Produced by Bob Crewe
Running Time: 83.20
Released in the US and the UK on Philips Records

SIDE ONE
Sherry (Gaudio)
Big Girls Don't Cry (Crewe/Gaudio)
Connie-O (Crewe/Gaudio)
Walk Like A Man (Crewe/Gaudio)
Candy Girl (Santos)
Marlena (Gaudio)
Peanuts (Guerrero)
Ain't That A Shame
(Domino/Bartholomew)

SIDE TWO
Dawn (Go Away) (Gaudio/Linzer)
Stay (Williams)
Big Man In Town (Gaudio)
Alone (Craft/Craft)
Save It For Me (Crewe/Gaudio)
Girl Come Running (Crewe/Gaudio)
Ronnie (Crewe/Gaudio)

SIDE THREE
Rag Doll (Crewe/Gaudio)
Bye Bye Baby (Baby Goodbye)
(Crewe/Gaudio)
Toy Soldier (Crewe/Gaudio)
Let's Hang On (Crewe/Randell/Linzer)
Don't Think Twice (by The Wonder Who)
(Dylan)
Working My Way Back To You
(Randell/Linzer)
Opus 17 (Don't Worry 'Bout Me)
(Randell/ Linzer)

SIDE FOUR
I've Got You Under My Skin (Porter)
Tell It To The Rain (Petrillo/Cifelli)
Beggin' (Crewe/Gaudio)
Silence Is Golden (Crewe/Gaudio)
C'mon Marianne (Brown/Bloodworth)
Watch The Flowers Grow
(Brown/Bloodworth)
Will You Still Love Me Tomorrow
(Goffin/King)

If The Beach Boys defined a West Coast sound in the '60s, Frankie Valli and his colleagues in The Four Seasons were simultaneously more consistent for a longer period with their sophisticated East Coast doo-wop.

After several years of dues paying, producer Bob Crewe decided in 1962 to use Valli's extraordinarily high vocal range – not falsetto, as has been suggested, since that cannot be sustained for as long or as loudly as Valli managed, seemingly effortlessly – on 'Sherry', a song written by group member Bob Gaudio.

It was the first of four US Number 1s and ten other US Top 10 hits they would notch up by early 1968.

This exemplary double album cannot be faulted other than perhaps for its anonymous sleeve. No group photograph appears on any part of its four surfaces – a ludicrous omission.

THE SEASONS' HARDY PERENNIALS

Apart from the UK chart-topping 'Silence Is Golden' by The Tremeloes, other acts also covered original tracks from this album and made the chart, including The Bay City Rollers and The Symbols (who both did 'Bye Bye Baby'), Timebox ('Beggin') and Donny Osmond ('C'mon Marianne'), while the group's ability to successfully revive hits from the past ('Ain't That A Shame', 'Alone', 'Stay', 'I've Got You Under My Skin', 'Will You Still Love Me Tomorrow' and others) must have made the Vee Jay label (on which many of these tracks were first released), the envy of the record industry (especially as Vee Jay also released the first Beatles album in the US – the label's inventive repackaging included a double album, The Beatles Vs. The Four Seasons, with a complete album by each group).

In 1967, The Four Seasons acquired ownership of their own past recordings after leaving Vee Jay due to non-payment of royalties, becoming one of the first acts to control its own destiny in this way.

GREATEST HITS

DONOVAN (1969)

SIDE ONE
Epistle To Dippy (D. Leitch)
Sunshine Superman (D. Leitch)
There Is A Mountain (D. Leitch)
Jennifer Juniper (D. Leitch)
Wear Your Love Like Heaven (D. Leitch)
Season Of The Witch (D. Leitch)

SIDE TWO
Mellow Yellow (D. Leitch)
Colours (D. Leitch)
Hurdy Gurdy Man (D. Leitch)
Catch The Wind (D. Leitch)
Lalena (D. Leitch)

Produced by Mickie Most
Total running time: 39.31
Released on Pye Records in the UK and Epic Records in the US

Scottish singer/songwriter Donovan Leitch, an icon of Swinging London, made numerous albums in the '60s. But this outstanding collection was the first LP on which his early hits were compiled with his later electric, but still folk-based, material.

It was his only US album to be certified platinum, but in the UK, where the earlier tracks had appeared on many budget albums, it was never listed in the chart. Unjustly dubbed the British Dylan – they shared a major influence in Woody Guthrie, hence the acoustic guitar and harmonica harness – Donovan was launched as a troubadour with simple folk songs like 'Catch The Wind' and 'Colours', but plugged his guitar in with the arrival of the golden-fingered producer Most.

Without fully abandoning the gentle approach (eg 'Jennifer Juniper', written about Jenny Boyd, who ran a stall known as Juniper in London's Portobello Road – her sister, Patti, married Beatle George Harrison, whom she left to marry Eric Clapton, while Jenny herself married Fleetwood Mac leader Mick Fleetwood), his other international hits included here bordered on acid rock.

'Sunshine Superman' was a captivating rock hymn to the times which topped the US chart, while 'Mellow Yellow', supposedly with a whispering vocal by Paul McCartney. was about a vibrator, according to Mickie Most, and made the US Top 3.

Most of the other tracks were substantial successes as singles, especially 'Hurdy Gurdy Man', a US Top 5 hit.

YOGI BARED

Donovan was one of many rock stars who during the later '60s became interested in the teachings of transcendental meditation guru Maharishi Mahesh Yogi, along with The Beatles, Mick Jagger, The Beach Boys and film star Mia Farrow.

Unlike many of that illustrious list, whose interest in the Maharishi lessened when they noticed during a visit to India in early 1968 that he was showing interest of a non-spiritual nature in female members of the all-star party (John Lennon's 'Sexy Sadie' was written about him), Donovan remained grateful for his inspiration, including a photograph of himself and The Maharishi on the sleeve of his 1968 double album, A Gift From A Flower To A Garden.

Donovan's status in the Swinging London hierarchy can be judged by the fact that he was a prominent member of the studio audience when The Beatles premiered 'All You Need Is Love' as part of the pioneering 'Our World', the first live international satellite TV show, which was screened around the world on 26 June 1967.

STAND !

SLY & THE FAMILY STONE (1969)

SIDE ONE
Stand! (S. Stewart)
Don't Call Me Nigger, Whitey (S. Stewart)
I Want To Take You Higher (S. Stewart)
Somebody's Watching You (S. Stewart)
Sing A Simple Song (S. Stewart)

SIDE TWO
Everyday People (S. Stewart)
Sex Machine (S. Stewart)
You Can Make It If You Try (S. Stewart)

Produced by Sly Stone for Stone Flower Productions
Total running time: 41.31
Released in the US by Epic Records and in the UK by Direction Records

Sly & The Family Stone, formed, fronted and led by vocalist, guitarist and keyboard player Sly Stone (real name Sylvester Stewart), were the pioneers of psychedelic soul during the second half of the '60s. This album is a striking example of the genre.

Based in Oakland, California, the multi-racial seven piece band mixed acid rock, funk, jazz, brassy R&B and other ingredients to produce a quite unique musical blend given an added sheen by their uninhibited stage show.

They soon became a locally popular part of San Francisco's psychedelic explosion in 1966.

This, the band's fourth album in two years, was hugely popular, remaining in the US album chart for almost two years and including two US hit singles, both of whose B-sides were also hit singles separately – 'Everyday People' topped the US chart and sold a million (and was a UK Top 40 hit), while 'Sing A Simple Song' was a minor US hit, after which the album's title track made the US Top 30 and its flipside, 'I Want To Take You Higher' came close to the US Top 50.

Flamboyant and outrageous, Sly Stone was the ringmaster of a circus of conflicting contrasts: the long (13 minute plus) self-explanatory 'Sex Machine' on the one hand and the black power cry of the title track and ironic political humour of 'Don't Call Me Nigger, Whitey' on the other.

With his highly skilled band, most of whom had played in several previous amateur groups, Stone and his band provided a sadly appropriate soundtrack to the end of the hippie dream.

STONED!

Sly Stone lived in Dallas, Texas, before moving to San Francisco in the '50s. On leaving school, he worked as a disc jockey on station KSOL, after which he became a producer for Autumn Records, a local label, with several notable clients.

Some sources also claim that he produced The Great Society, featuring Grace Slick, later of Jefferson Airplane. After playing with a group called The Mojo Men, he formed The Stoners, a shortlived group which also included trumpeter Cynthia Robinson, with whom he launched Sly & The Family Stone with his brother, Freddie, on lead guitar, his sister, Rosie, on keyboards, a remarkable bass player in Larry Graham, sax player Jerry Martini and drummer Greg Errico, later a founder member of Journey.

The group's almost continual brushes with the law over drugs contributed to their swift decline from US chart-toppers – with the classic album There's A Riot Goin' On in 1971 – to chart-strugglers just three years later.

They were not allowed to perform during their first UK visit in 1968, because customs officers had discovered cannabis in a group member's luggage – and despite a stunning performance of 'I Want To Take You Higher' at the Woodstock Festival, the group were known to be unreliable. They missed over 30% of their 80 booked shows in 1970.

DUSTY IN MEMPHIS

DUSTY SPRINGFIELD (1969)

SIDE ONE
Just A Little Lovin' (Mann/Weil)
So Much Love (Goffin/King)
Son Of A Preacher Man (Hurley/Wilkins)
I Don't Want To Hear It Anymore
(Newman)
Don't Forget About Me (Goffin/King)

SIDE TWO
Breakfast In Bed (Hinton/Fritts)
Just One Smile (Newman)
The Windmills Of Your Mind
(Bergman/LeGrand/Bergman)
In The Land Of Make Believe
(Bacharach/David)
No Easy Way Down (Goffin/King)
I Can't Make It Alone (Goffin/King)

Produced by Jerry Wexler, Tom Dowd & Arif Mardin
Total running time: 32.56
Released in the UK by Philips Records and in the US by Atlantic Records

One of the UK's most admired female vocalists, Dusty Springfield had enjoyed a long succession of hit singles since 'I Only Want To Be With You', her 1963 Top 10 debut.

But her often-stated affection for black R&B music (particularly Motown and Stax/Atlantic) had rarely, if ever, been reflected in the way she made her records. Not that they were commercial flops – they weren't – but they lacked the soulful informality of US R&B records.

In London the instrumental backing and arrangements would be complete perhaps days before she added her vocal. In the US everyone involved in a record (musicians, producer, engineer and vocalist) worked together to find the best approach. The chance to work in an organic rather than manufactured

manner in Memphis with producers from Atlantic Records (to whom she had just signed after dissatisfaction with her previous US label) was a dream come true for Dusty, and the first result, 'Son Of A Preacher Man', was a Top 10 single on both sides of the Atlantic.

Throughout the album, she sounds relaxed and at ease, and it is widely regarded as the finest of her career, combining four songs from the prolific husband and wife team, Gerry Goffin & Carole King, who had written two of her best loved hits, 'Some Of Your Lovin'' and 'Going Back', and another by Burt Bacharach & Hal David, three of whose songs had given her previous hits.

Her best song ever, 'Breakfast In Bed', is also included. The album only just reached the US Top 100, but it stayed there longer than any of her others.

SINGULAR FAME

Dusty Springfield first recorded as a 20-year-old in the vocal trio The Lana Sisters, but her first taste of stardom came when she formed a trio in 1961 with her brother, Tom Springfield (real name Dion O'Brien), and Tim Field. Also adopting her professional alias at this time, Dusty (real name Mary O'Brien) was the focal point of The Springfields, who concentrated on country and folk material and scored five UK hits in two years plus a US Top 20 single, 'Silver Threads & Golden Needles', before Dusty's solo ambitions led to its dissolution in late 1963.

Her first solo single, 1964's 'I Only Want To Be With You', was a UK Top 5/US Top 20 hit (which incidentally was the first record ever played on the long-running UK TV chart show, 'Top Of The Pops', on 1 January 1964). This solo debut marked a distinct change in musical style, with its obvious nod to Motown influence, and this approach continued throughout the '60s with superb albums like A Girl Called Dusty (1964) and Everything's Coming Up Dusty (1965), both of which predominantly featured songs by American writers.

TOMMY

THE WHO (1969)

Produced by Kit Lambert
Total running time: 74.58
*Released in the UK by Track Records and in
the US by Decca Records*

Pete Townshend's finest achievement, *Tommy* was the first internationally acclaimed 'rock opera'. It took the idea of a so-called 'concept' album to a logical conclusion (although not necessarily to a satisfactory plot denouement), and as such remains remarkable.

By 1969, The Who were established as one of the top groups in the world, just behind The Beatles and The Stones, but were still primarily seen as a singles act, particularly in the US, where only one of their LPs had made the Top 40.

Additionally, the group needed a different climax for their stage show to replace the instrument destruction and stage demolition which had made them internationally famous but had become an immense financial drain.

This was Townshend's chance to not only allow the group to escape the vast expense, which was no longer necessary, but also to elevate them to the premier league, and he spent many months conceiving a plot (about a deaf, dumb and blind boy) and writing songs which not only told a story but often stood on their own merits.

'Pinball Wizard' (UK Top 5/US Top 20) is the stand-out song here, and was also a UK Top 10 hit in 1976 for Elton John, who played the part of the pinball wizard in the movie version of 'Tommy', directed by Ken Russell. Roger Daltrey took the title role and his interpretations of songs like 'See Me, Feel Me' gave his vocals an extra dimension.

SIDE ONE
Overture (Pete Townshend)
It's A Boy (Pete Townshend)
1921 (Pete Townshend)
Amazing Journey (Pete Townshend)
Sparks (Pete Townshend)
Eyesight To The Blind (The Hawker)
(Sonny Boy Williamson)

SIDE TWO
Christmas (Pete Townshend)
Cousin Kevin (John Entwistle)
The Acid Queen (Pete Townshend)
Underture (Pete Townshend)

SIDE THREE
Do You Think It's Alright (Pete Townshend)
Fiddle About (John Entwistle)
Pinball Wizard (Pete Townshend)
There's A Doctor (Pete Townshend)
Go To The Mirror (Pete Townshend)
Tommy Can You Hear Me?
(Pete Townshend)
Smash The Mirror (Pete Townshend)
Sensation (Pete Townshend)

SIDE FOUR
Miracle Cure (Pete Townshend)
Sally Simpson (Pete Townshend)
I'm Free (Pete Townshend)
Welcome (Pete Townshend)
Tommy's Holiday Camp (Keith Moon)
We're Not Gonna Take It (Pete Townshend)

WHO'S BEST?

As well as the acclaim he received for Tommy, *Pete Townshend was also successful as a producer when 'Something In The Air' by Thunderclap Newman, an unlikely trio of a middle-aged (in looks and approach) jazz pianist, a singing drummer and a teenage guitarist, topped the UK chart.*

The Who's brilliant performance at Woodstock was widely regarded as one of the highlights of the festival, and Townshend had achieved his aim of elevating the group's status. After an eventful 1970, during which Moon accidentally killed his chauffeur by running over him in his car, the group's follow-up album was Live At Leeds, *recorded at Leeds University, which was a UK Top 3/US Top 50 hit, but was clearly a holding action until Townshend could create an appropriate follow-up to* Tommy. *Their next album, 1971's* Who's Next, *was their finest ever.*

WITH A LITTLE HELP FROM MY FRIENDS

JOE COCKER(1969)

SIDE ONE
Feeling Alright (Dave Mason)
Bye Bye Blackbird (Henderson/Dixon)
Change In Louise
(Joe Cocker/Chris Stainton)
Marjorine (Joe Cocker/Chris Stainton/
Tom Rattigan/Frank Myles)
Just Like A Woman (Bob Dylan)

SIDE TWO
Do I Still Figure In Your Life (Peter Dello)
Sandpaper Cadillac
(Joe Cocker/Chris Stainton)
Don't Let Me Be Misunderstood
(B. Benjamin/G. Caldwell/S. Marcus)
With A Little Help From My Friends
(John Lennon/Paul McCartney)
I Shall Be Released (Bob Dylan)

Produced by Denny Cordell for
Straight Ahead Productions
Total running time: 41.16
Released in the UK on Regal-Zonophone Records and in the US on A&M Records

Undoubtedly a classic, this first album by the erstwhile gas fitter from Sheffield has been the blueprint for the majority of his subsequent album output.

A highlight was Cocker's radical approach (which he said he conceived in the toilet of his parent's home) to the track from the *Sergeant Pepper* album.

With a trio of female backing singers, Jimmy Page on lead guitar and B.J. Wilson of Procol Harum behind the drums, 'With A Little Help' topped the UK singles chart at the end of 1968 to become Cocker's second UK hit.

Recorded in London and Los Angeles, the album featured several other big names working as session musicians. These included Stev(i)e Winwood, who played organ on 'Do I Still Figure' and the final Dylan song; Wilson's Procol Harum colleague Matthew Fisher, who played organ on 'Just Like A Woman'; Tornados drummer Clem Cattini (drums on three tracks) and the ubiquitous Chris Stainton, Cocker's songwriting partner, who played bass on nine tracks, and organ and/or piano on four of the nine.

Guitarist Albert Lee, the British country star, appears on 'Marjorine'.

GOOD INFLUENCES

Cocker and his backing group of the mid-'60s first recorded in 1964 as Vance Arnold & The Avengers. Their sole release, a cover of a Beatles song from A Hard Day's Night, 'I'll Cry Instead', was a total flop, despite Jimmy Page playing on it.

Cocker's major international breakthrough came with his appearance at the Woodstock festival in 1969, when his apparently unco-ordinated physical performance involving playing an imaginary guitar, together with a soulful voice which seemed to properly belong to someone with a black skin, made him an instant sensation. His greatest influence was Ray Charles, and many years later, in the '80s, he finally achieved his lifelong ambition by sharing a duet with his mentor. Of greater significance to this album is the fact that its opening track, a cover version of a song by Dave Mason (then of Traffic, Steve Winwood's band), was recorded at A&M Studios in Los Angeles using exclusively American musicians, among whom were three female backing vocalists, Brenda Holloway, Merry Clayton and Patrice Holloway. At the time, they also worked with Ray Charles as his vocal backing trio, The Raelettes.

Joe Cocker did not return to the top of the charts until 1982, when his duet with Jennifer Warnes, 'Up Where We Belong', as featured in the successful movie, 'An Officer And A Gentleman', starring Richard Gere & Debra Winger, was Number 1 on both sides of the Atlantic.

CROSBY, STILLS & NASH

CROSBY, STILLS & NASH (1969)

SIDE ONE
Suite: Judy Blue Eyes (Stephen Stills)
Marrakesh Express (Graham Nash)
Guinnevere (David Crosby)
You Don't Have To Cry (Stephen Stills)
Pre-Road Downs (Graham Nash)

SIDE TWO
Wooden Ships (David Crosby/Stephen Stills)
Lady Of The Island (Graham Nash)
Helplessly Hoping (Stephen Stills)
Long Time Gone (David Crosby)
49 Bye-Byes (Stephen Stills)

*Produced by David Crosby, Stephen Stills,
Graham Nash*
Total running time: 40.43
Released in the US & UK by Atlantic Records

This much anticipated debut album from one of the first 'supergroups' lived up to all their fans' expectations.

David Crosby, who had left The Byrds because of conflicts over musical direction, knew Stephen Stills, one of three songwriters in Buffalo Springfield, who had broken up in disarray.

During a party thrown by 'Mama' Cass (of The Mamas & Papas), they began to sing with Englishman Graham Nash, a member of The Hollies, and discovered that their vocal harmonies blended beautifully.

This was the first recorded result, and was well-received on both sides of the Atlantic, reaching the US Top 10 and UK Top 30 and spawning a US & UK Top 30 single, Nash's 'Marrakesh Express', and a superb follow-up which nearly made the US Top 20, Stills' heartfelt love song to Judy Collins, 'Suite: Judy Blue Eyes'.

There was a question mark over the three band members' instrumental capabilities — the sleeve picture shows Stills with a guitar, and his colleagues empty-handed. This was reflected on the album, with Stills playing lead guitar, organ and bass, Crosby credited with rhythm guitar, and Nash with nothing in terms of instruments.

Nash's 'Lady Of The Island' was written about two different people, one from Ibiza and the other from Long Island, while the assassination of Bobby Kennedy inspired Crosby to write 'Long Time Gone'. Stills's '49 Bye-Byes' was originally two songs, '49 Reasons' and 'Bye-Bye Baby'.

CONTRACT FACTS

Before Crosby, Stills & Nash could record together, certain contractual problems had to be ironed out. Buffalo Springfield were signed to Atlantic Records and Graham Nash was contracted in the US to Epic, a Columbia (CBS)-related label, with The Hollies.

Ahmet Ertegun, founder of Atlantic Records, wanted to sign the trio, but before he could do so, he had to arrange compensation for Columbia losing Nash.

That was achieved by freeing Richie Furay, another ex-member of Buffalo Springfield, from his obligations to Atlantic and allowing him to take his new group, Poco, to Epic. Crosby was the only free agent at the time, as he had been replaced in The Byrds, who continued to record with new members, notably Gram Parsons.

One of the first big live shows played by Crosby, Stills & Nash was the Woodstock Festival. It was clear by then that they needed more instrumental weight, so Stills invited Neil Young, yet another ex-Buffalo Springfield member, to join as an additional lead guitarist.

The group's 1970 album, Deja Vu, which topped the US chart, was by CSN&Y (Crosby, Stills, Nash & Young). All four band members pooled their songwriting resources for that album, which was another musical masterpiece.

CLOUDS

JONI MITCHELL (1969)

Produced by Joni Mitchell & Henry Lewy, except * produced by Paul Rothchild

SIDE ONE
Tin Angel (Joni Mitchell)*
Chelsea Morning (Joni Mitchell)
I Don't Know Where I Stand (Joni Mitchell)
That Song About The Midway
(Joni Mitchell)
Roses Blue (Joni Mitchell)

SIDE TWO
The Gallery (Joni Mitchell)
I Think I Understand (Joni Mitchell)
Songs To Aging Children Come
(Joni Mitchell)
The Fiddle And The Drum (Joni Mitchell)
Both Sides, Now (Joni Mitchell)

Total running time: 36.52
Released in the US & UK by Reprise Records

Canadian Joni Mitchell was working at the Cafe Au GoGo in Greenwich Village, New York, in 1966 when she attracted the attention of agent Elliot Roberts. He signed her to a management deal after seeing her opening for Richie Havens.

At that stage, her main thrust was as a songwriter – Tom Rush, who had seen her perform in Detroit, spread the word in New York of her songwriting prowess and in 1967 Al Kooper, whom she met at the Cafe Au GoGo, recommended her to his friend, Judy Collins, who covered two Mitchell compositions, 'Michael From Mountains' and 'Both Sides Now', on her album *Wildflowers*.

After that, Tom Rush covered three of her songs on his 1968 album, *The Circle Game*: 'Urge For Going', the title track and 'Tin Angel', the opening track

on this, her second album. UK folk/rock band Fairport Convention covered 'I Don't Know Where I Stand' and 'Chelsea Morning' on their eponymous 1968 debut album.

So by the time Joni Mitchell began releasing records on her own account as a singer/songwriter, accompanying herself on guitar and piano, her name was familiar among discriminating contemporary folk fans, although her debut album, produced by David Crosby, while a critical success, only just reached the US chart.

When *Clouds* was released in late 1969, she was almost a household name (especially as the Judy Collins version of 'Both Sides Now' had become a US Top 10 single), and the album was a substantial US hit, almost making the Top 30. Collins also had a hit with Mitchell's 'Chelsea Morning'.

POETIC PASSION

The abiding impression left by the lyrics of many of Joni Mitchell's best-known songs is one of consummate poetry. Their precise meaning is not always obvious, although her more accessible songs, such as her glorious evocation of the parallels between romance and the sky in 'Both Sides Now', and the joyful 'Chelsea Morning' (doubtless inspired by a period in 1967 when she lived in London), are more straightforward and obviously superior to the songs of most of her contemporaries.

Ironically, her most commercially successful song, 'Woodstock', concerns an event which she did not attend – she was living with Graham Nash (of Crosby, Stills & Nash) at the time, and was booked to play on the bill of the famous festival, but on the advice of David Geffen, her co-manager, appeared instead on a TV show. She wrote the song shortly afterwards, and included it on her third album, Ladies Of The Canyon, released in 1970. That album also included her only UK hit single, 'Big Yellow Taxi', one of the first ecological protest songs.

EVERYBODY KNOWS THIS IS NOWHERE

NEIL YOUNG & CRAZY HORSE (1969)

SIDE ONE
Cinnamon Girl (Neil Young)
Everybody Knows This Is Nowhere
(Neil Young)
Round And Round (It Won't Be Long)
(Neil Young)
Down By The River (Neil Young)

SIDE TWO
The Losing End (When You're On)
(Neil Young)
Running Dry (Requiem For The Rockets)
(Neil Young)
Cowgirl In The Sand (Neil Young)

Produced by David Briggs & Neil Young Total running time: 40.31
Released in the US and UK by Reprise Records

This timeless epic, Neil Young's second solo album, was his first to fully realise the promise he had earlier shown with Buffalo Springfield.

When the Springfield imploded, Young decided on a solo career, releasing an eponymous debut album in early 1969, which met with little acclaim. During the album sessions, Young met The Rockets, a Los Angeles quartet, whom he invited to back him on this LP, which has remained one of the prolific Young's best-loved albums.

Ex-Rockets Danny Whitten (guitar), Billy Talbot (bass) and Ralph Molina (drums) (now renamed Crazy Horse) played throughout this album, while the fourth ex-Rocket, violinist Bobby Notkoff, appropriately appears on 'Running Dry'.

'Round And Round' features Robin Lane's vocals, but this was Young's album. It included the first widely-heard examples of his simple but highly effective one note guitar solos, where the timing and the backing blend to create a strange magic that is peculiar to the Canadian superstar.

The final track on each side is an epic, 'Down By The River' lasting over nine minutes and 'Cowgirl' ten and a half, both in truth being little more than a short and simple framework used as the starting point for a monumental guitar solo by Young.

Both remain tracks by which Young's often staggering subsequent compositions are judged. They may not be his absolute best songs but they are among his most memorable.

YOUNG TALENT

Born in Toronto in 1945, Neil Young is the son of noted Canadian sports journalist Scott Young (who later wrote a biography of his son). Neil achieved local fame on the Canadian folk circuit, leading Neil Young & The Squires, his first group of note, in the early '60s. He then joined The Mynah Birds, led by black vocalist Rick James, a deserter from the US Navy until the long arm of the law apprehended James and forced him to return to the forces to serve his time.

Young then drove to Los Angeles, hoping to renew his acquaintance with Stephen Stills, and, in early 1966, joined Stills as a founder member of Buffalo Springfield. The tempestuous relationships among the members of the group resulted in Young leaving and rejoining on several occasions before the group finally collapsed in May 1968.

His first solo album, part-produced by Jack Nitzsche (assisted by Ry Cooder) and partly by David Briggs, was released in early 1969. Stills, meanwhile, had formed Crosby, Stills & Nash, whose debut album was a million-seller, but whose instrumental power depended heavily on Stills. He persuaded Young to join after some negotiation over billing — the result was one of the era's best supergroups, Crosby, Stills, Nash & Young.

UNHALFBRICKING

FAIRPORT CONVENTION (1969)

SIDE ONE
Genesis Hall (Richard Thompson)
Si Tu Dois Partir (Bob Dylan)
Autopsy (Sandy Denny)
A Sailor's Life (Trad. arr. Fairport)

SIDE TWO
Cajun Woman (Richard Thompson)
Who Knows Where The Time Goes
(Sandy Denny)
Percy's Song (Bob Dylan)
Million Dollar Bash (Bob Dylan)

Produced by Joe Boyd, Simon Nicol and Fairport Convention
Total running time: 39.47
Released in the UK on Island Records and in the US on A&M Records

This was Fairport's finest achievement. With the group's early leading lights: songwriters Richard Thompson (lead guitar and vocals) and Sandy Denny (lead vocal, guitar, piano) plus Ashley Hutchings (bass), in full accord, Fairport, which also included at that time guitarist Simon Nicol and drummer Martin Lamble, covered three Bob Dylan songs (then still to be released by the latter) and completed the album with four originals and a radical approach to the traditional epic, 'A Sailor's Life'.

Thompson and Denny introduced stunning originals like 'Genesis Hall' and 'Who Knows Where The Time Goes' respectively, and the group decided to translate the lyrics of Dylan's 'If You Gotta Go, Go Now', a big 1965 hit for Manfred Mann, into French.

Surprisingly, in view of their deserved reputation as the world's finest folk/rock band, Fairport's only UK hit single was this song, 'Si Tu Dois Partir'.

Denny had already recorded 'Who Knows Where The Time Goes' during her membership of The Strawbs, a group she left to join Fairport, but internationally the best-known version of this fine song was by American folk star Judy Collins.

Unhalfbricking was released only weeks after all the group apart from Denny were involved in a serious road accident on a motorway just north of London, which resulted in the death of 19-year-old Lamble, although the rest of the group survived relatively unscathed.

The middle-aged couple who are featured on the sleeve of this album are Sandy Denny's parents, and the garden in front of which they are standing belonged to their home in Wimbledon, south-west London.

Tragically, Denny died of a brain haemorrhage in 1978.

A RETURN TO FOLK CONVENTION

The group called itself Fairport after the name of a house in North London in which Ashley Hutchings was living in a rented room, and in which Simon Nicol, a doctor's son, had coincidentally lived a few years before, when it was used as a doctor's surgery. The third album by Fairport Convention, Unhalfbricking (a title resulting from a word game) was also the first by the group on which noted folk fiddler Dave Swarbrick played, although as a session musician.

Lamble was replaced by Dave Mattacks for 1970's Liege & Lief on which the material was predominantly traditional (and had been discovered after research by Ashley Hutchings at Cecil Sharp House, the London headquarters of the English Folk Dance & Song Society). Soon after Liege & Lief, Hutchings and Sandy Denny both left the band, Denny because she regarded Liege & Lief as an experiment and wanted the band to revert to its previous more contemporary approach, and Hutchings because he felt the traditional songs on Liege & Lief should have sparked the start of an exciting new musical direction for the band.

ARETHA'S GOLD

ARETHA FRANKLIN (1969)

SIDE ONE
I Never Loved A Man (The Way I Love You)
(Ronnie Shannon)
Do Right Woman – Do Right Man
(Dan Penn/Chips Moman)
Respect (Otis Redding)
Dr. Feelgood (Aretha Franklin/Ted White)
Baby, I Love You (Ronnie Shannon)
(You Make Me Feel Like) A Natural Woman
(Gerry Goffin/Carole King/Jerry Wexler)
Chain Of Fools (Don Covay)

SIDE TWO
Since You've Been Gone (Sweet Sweet Baby)
(Aretha Franklin/Ted White)
Ain't No Way (Carolyn Franklin/Ted White)
Think (Aretha Franklin, Ted White)
You Send Me (Sam Cooke)
The House That Jack Built
(Bob Lance/Fran Robins)
I Say A Little Prayer
(Burt Bacharach/Hal David)
See Saw (Steve Cropper/Don Covay)

Produced by Jerry Wexler
Total running time: 39.34
Released in the US & UK by Atlantic Records

t the age of 18, gospel singer Aretha Franklin moved to New York to pursue a career in secular music, and was quickly signed by legendary talent scout John Hammond to Columbia Records.

However, her Columbia releases were mainly jazz-oriented, and few made a significant chart impact. So she left the label during 1966 and moved to Atlantic at producer Jerry Wexler's instigation, immediately starting the run of classics collected on this album.

Her first three Atlantic singles of 1967, 'I Never Loved A Man', her superb cover of Otis Redding's 'Respect' (her first US chart-topper) and 'Baby I Love You', each sold a million. In 1968, 'Chain Of Fools', 'Since You've Been Gone', 'Think', 'I Say A Little Prayer' and 'See Saw', also went gold.

Aretha wrote some of these soul classics, collaborating with her husband/manager, Ted White. He also wrote 'Ain't No Way' with her sister, Carolyn Franklin.

Among the musicians who supplied the solid backing were guitarists Jimmy Johnson, Tommy Cogbill and (on a few tracks) Duane Allman, bass player Jerry Jemmott and drummer Roger Hawkins. The horn section included Wayne Jackson and Andrew Love (of The Memphis Horns) and Curtis Ousley.

Most of those musicians were from the South, but they came to New York (for the majority of these sessions) to capture the flavour of Aretha's roots while using the latest recording technology.

SOUL SISTERS

Born in Memphis, Tennessee, Aretha Franklin was one of six children raised by their father after their mother deserted the family when Aretha was under ten years old. Two of her younger sisters, Erma and Carolyn, were also recording artists in their own right, and while neither was remotely as successful as Aretha, Erma was the first artist to chart with 'Piece Of My Heart', which later became the breakthrough hit for Janis Joplin as vocalist of Big Brother & The Holding Company.

Aretha accumulated nine US pop hits and six more which made the R&B chart during her unhappy six years with Columbia, but the only one to reach the Top 40 at that time was her cover of the Al Jolson standard, 'Rock-A-Bye Your Baby With A Dixie Melody', which was typical of the general unsuitability of the material she was given to record.

Everything changed when she moved to Atlantic, and in the final three years of the decade, 22 of her singles were US pop hits, 14 of them making the Top 20. In the 1967-1969 period, she released two LPs per year, three of which went gold and all of which reached the US Top 20, as did Aretha's Gold.

BLIND FAITH

BLIND FAITH (1969)

SIDE ONE
Had To Cry Today (S. Winwood)
Can't Find My Way Home (S. Winwood)
Well All Right
(N. Petty/B. Holly/J. Allison/J. Mauldin)

SIDE TWO
Presence Of The Lord (E. Clapton)
Sea Of Joy (S. Winwood)
Do What You Like (G. Baker)

Produced by Jimmy Miller
Total running time: 41.54
Released in the UK by Polydor Records and
in the US by Atco Records

Following the demise of Cream, the original so-called supergroup, guitarist Eric Clapton wanted to work with vocalist/keyboard player Steve Winwood, leader of Traffic.

The result was Blind Faith, and this short-lived experiment produced an album of progressive rock that captured the musical mood of the times. That was reflected in *Blind Faith* topping the charts on both sides of the Atlantic.

Clapton and Winwood had recorded together in Eric Clapton & The Powerhouse, a studio group, in 1966, but had subsequently rarely been able to collaborate. Cream's collapse gave them the chance they needed.

After managers Robert Stigwood (for Clapton) and Chris Blackwell (for Winwood) had agreed to allow their charges to record together, they needed an equally notable rhythm section. Clapton's ex-Cream colleague, drummer

Peter 'Ginger' Baker, was available, and although some felt that using Baker made the new group little more than a reformed Cream, he was invited to join. Bass player Ric Grech had been in Family, a group from Leicester which had been fairly successful in Europe without making an impression in the US.

Blind Faith recorded their only LP in the first half of 1969, and played their only UK gig at a free concert in London's Hyde Park, prior to a sell-out US stadium tour, after which they broke up on the grounds that the group was musically unsatisfying.

The Winwood songs were fine, as was the Buddy Holly cover, but Baker's drum feature was over-lengthy at 15 minutes plus. Clapton's neo-religious item was the major highlight of an album which remains historic, not least because it proved that the sum of the parts of this supergroup amounted to rather more than the whole.

LOST FAITH

Clapton was already disenchanted with Blind Faith during the group's US tour, spending more time with the opening act, Delaney & Bonnie & Friends, than with his own colleagues. When the tour was over and Blind Faith was a thing of the past, Clapton joined Delaney & Bonnie's group for a US tour which he apparently helped to finance, appearing on a live album, Delaney & Bonnie With Eric Clapton On Tour.

He was also a member of John Lennon's Plastic Ono Band, on whose hit single, 'Cold Turkey', he had guested, for their first ever live concert in Canada on 13 September 1969. It was recorded and released as the Live Peace In Toronto LP.

Ultimately, the idea of Blind Faith was misconceived – one of the reasons for Cream's dissolution was that its members, particularly Clapton, were tired of the pressure of international fame, and with Blind Faith, that pressure increased. The sleeve picture was long believed to feature Baker's daughter, but in fact is of an anonymous child model.

AOXOMOXOA

THE GRATEFUL DEAD (1969)

Produced by The Grateful Dead
Total running time: 36.13
Released in the US & UK by Warner Bros.
Records

SIDE ONE
St. Stephen
(Robert Hunter/Jerry Garcia/Phil Lesh)
Dupree's Diamond Blues
(Robert Hunter/Jerry Garcia/Phil Lesh)
Rosemary
(Robert Hunter/Jerry Garcia/Phil Lesh)
Doin' That Rag
(Robert Hunter/Jerry Garcia/Phil Lesh)
Mountains Of The Moon
(Robert Hunter/Jerry Garcia/Phil Lesh)

SIDE TWO
China Cat Sunflower
(Robert Hunter/Jerry Garcia/Phil Lesh)
What's Become Of The Baby
(Robert Hunter/Jerry Garcia/Phil Lesh)
Cosmic Charlie
(Robert Hunter/Jerry Garcia/Phil Lesh)

T he Grateful Dead were one of the first and most influential groups in the first wave of the psychedelic movement which had started in San Francisco during the mid-'60s.

The group's central figure was Jerome 'Jerry' Garcia, vocalist, lead guitarist and chief songwriter in collaboration with bass player/vocalist Phil Lesh and lyricist Robert Hunter, who was not a performing member of the band.

The group initially became famous for their lengthy live shows, when the almost telepathic relationship between the group members led to single songs often lasting 20 minutes or more.

This magic wasn't easy to capture in the recording studio, as the group's fans discovered when their first two albums, *Grateful Dead* (1967) and *Anthem Of The Sun* (1968) were released.

Aoxomoxoa was more successful in distilling the flavour of the live gigs, and with its brilliantly coloured hallucinogenic sleeve (the work of noted poster artist Rick Griffin) and its palindromic title, the album bore all the hallmarks of a psychedelic masterpiece.

It was a step forward from the previous albums, but such live concert favourites as the rocking 'St. Stephen' and the gentler 'China Cat Sunflower', inevitably lacked the interplay that was present when both audience and musicians were often under the influence of mind-expanding drugs such as LSD and marijuana.

THE LIVING DEAD

Unlike most of the groups in this book, The Grateful Dead remained active in the '90s. If anything, their popularity had increased.

They originally evolved from Mother McCree's Uptown Jug Champions, a San Francisco jug band whose members included the guitarists Jerry Garcia and Bob Weir, and the keyboard player Ron 'Pigpen' McKernan.

The trio launched The Warlocks in late 1964 with drummer Bill Kreutzmann. With the arrival of bass player Phil Lesh, this final version of The Warlocks was the initial line-up of The Grateful Dead, who recorded two albums worth of live material in 1966. Those albums were intended to form part of a ten LP set of live material recorded along with other psychedelic bands at San Francisco's Avalon Ballroom, although only the two albums by The Dead were ever released, as Vintage Dead (with an 18 minute version of Wilson Pickett's 'In The Midnight Hour') and Historic Dead in 1970/71.

Three Grateful Dead keyboard players died prematurely – 'Pigpen' in 1973 of over-indulgence in alcohol, his replacement Keith Godchaux in 1980 after a motorcycle accident and his replacement, Brent Mydland, of a drug overdose in 1990.

STAND UP

JETHRO TULL (1969)

SIDE ONE
A New Day Yesterday (Ian Anderson)
Jeffrey Goes To Leicester Square
(Ian Anderson)
Bouree (Bach, arranged by Ian Anderson)
Back To The Family (Ian Anderson)
Look Into The Sun (Ian Anderson)

SIDE TWO
Nothing Is Easy (Ian Anderson)
Fat Man (Ian Anderson)
We Need To Know (Ian Anderson)
Reasons For Waiting (Ian Anderson)
For A Thousand Mothers (Ian Anderson)

Produced by Terry Ellis & Ian Anderson
Total running time: 37.58
Released in the UK by Island Records and in
the US by Reprise Records

Stand Up's spectacular packaging – a gatefold sleeve with caricatures of the group which actually stand up when the sleeve is opened – helped it to enter the UK chart at Number 1, a considerable achievement in the '60s for a relatively new band.

In addition, leader Ian Anderson had developed his idiosyncratic and crowd-pleasing trademark of standing on one leg while frantically playing his flute in front of the R&B based backing of the rest of the group. Anderson's lightness of touch on the flute, allied to the heavy backing, made the Jethro Tull sound both original and irresistible.

Named after the 18th Century British inventor of the seed drill, Jethro Tull formed (originally as The Blades) in 1963 in the north-western English coastal resort of Blackpool.

They changed their name to John Evan's Smash in 1966. The group moved to London in 1967, but only vocalist/flautist Ian Anderson and Glenn Cornick (bass) felt able to withstand the hardships of life away from home.

After recruiting guitarist Mick Abrahams and drummer Clive Bunker from a small-time suburban R&B band, McGregor's Engine, the renamed quartet signed with London agency Chrysalis.

Acclaimed performances at a free concert in London supporting Pink Floyd and at the 1968 National Jazz & Blues festival attracted Island Records, who released their debut album, *This Was*, which made the UK Top 10.

After major disagreements in late 1968 between Anderson and Abrahams over leadership of the group and its future musical direction, Abrahams formed his own group, Blodwyn Pig.

BLACKPOOL ROCK

Before they recorded This Was, *the group had released a single, 'Sunshine Day' (written by Mick Abrahams), which was not a hit and was mistakenly credited to Jethro Toe. When Jethro Tull became successful, Anderson tightened his grip on the group, with regular changes of personnel involving everyone apart from Martin Barre (who replaced Mick Abrahams on guitar in early 1969) and Anderson himself, who at the start of the '70s often hired replacements for departing musicians from his earliest group in Blackpool.*

Between mid-1971 and the end of 1975, Jethro Tull released five consecutive gold albums, including two, Thick As A Brick *and* A Passion Play, *which topped the US chart.*

In 1972, Chrysalis had expanded from an agency into a record company. Jethro Tull were one of its first signings, and the group remained signed to that label over 20 years (and 19 hit albums) later, fronted as ever by Anderson (still playing the flute while standing on one leg), and with the faithful Barre on guitar.

ABBEY ROAD

THE BEATLES (1969)

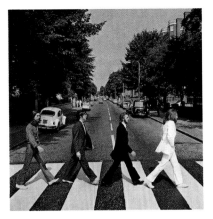

Produced by George Martin
Total running time: 47.26
Released in the UK by Apple/Parlophone
Records and in the US by Capitol Records

SIDE ONE
Come Together (Lennon/McCartney)
Something (Harrison)
Maxwell's Silver Hammer
(Lennon/McCartney)
Oh! Darling (Lennon/McCartney)
Octopus's Garden (Starkey)
I Want You (She's So Heavy)
(Lennon/McCartney)

SIDE TWO
Here Comes The Sun (Harrison)
Because (Lennon/McCartney)
You Never Give Me Your Money
(Lennon/McCartney)
Sun King (Lennon/McCartney)
Mean Mr. Mustard (Lennon/McCartney)
Polythene Pam (Lennon/McCartney)
She Came In Through The Bathroom Window
(Lennon/McCartney)
Golden Slumbers (Lennon/McCartney)
Carry That Weight (Lennon/McCartney)
The End (Lennon/McCartney)
Her Majesty (Lennon/McCartney)

fter the excesses of the double white album in 1968, *Abbey Road* came as a great relief. Producer George Martin had become disillusioned by the infighting that had become a feature of The Beatles' recording sessions in the late '60s and told them he would only work with them if they sorted themselves out.

The result was a return to the type of crisp songwriting that had made them so popular in the first place. In particular, the medley that took up most of side two was humorous and sharp.

The melody of Lennon's dreamy 'Because' was apparently inspired by Yoko Ono playing Beethoven piano chords backwards.

One verse of McCartney's 'Golden Slumbers' was 'borrowed' from the traditional nursery rhyme, and the 23 seconds long 'Her Majesty' was his tribute to Queen Elizabeth II – by the mid-'90s he had yet to be granted a knighthood...

Although it was not the last original LP by The Beatles to be released – *Let It Be* appeared in mid-1970 – this was the last LP by the Fab Four to be recorded. It topped the UK chart for 17 weeks and the US chart for 11.

It has sold over ten million copies worldwide. Its immediate popularity probably accounted for the fact that the UK single coupling 'Come Together' and 'Something' failed to top the chart. In the US, the two tracks respectively reached Number 1 and the Top 3.

FUNEREAL FEET

The Abbey Road LP sleeve played a significant part in the bizarre rumour which circulated in late 1969 suggesting that Paul McCartney had been replaced by a lookalike after his death in a 1966 car accident, and that the surviving Beatles had been providing subtle clues which would break the sad news to their fans before a formal announcement.

The sleeve, showing the group crossing the street near the studio, was interpreted as a funeral party, with John Lennon (the preacher) leading the way, Ringo behind him as a mourner, Paul (significantly barefooted, as in some places corpses are buried without shoes) as the deceased and George as the gravedigger, while the number plate on the white Volkswagen includes '281F', and Paul would have been 28 if he had survived...

The four months of recording Abbey Road began in April 1969, shortly after McCartney and Lennon had respectively married Linda Eastman and Yoko Ono within eight days of each other, the McCartneys plighting their troth at Marylebone registry office in London, the Lennons at the British consulate in Gibraltar.

GREEN RIVER

CREEDENCE CLEARWATER REVIVAL (1969)

SIDE ONE
Green River (J. C. Fogerty)
Commotion (J. C. Fogerty)
Tombstone Shadow (J. C. Fogerty)
Wrote A Song For Everyone (J. C. Fogerty)
Bad Moon Rising (J. C. Fogerty)

SIDE TWO
Lodi (J. C. Fogerty)
Cross-Tie Walker (J. C. Fogerty)
Sinister Purpose (J. C. Fogerty)
Night Time Is The Right Time (Herman)

Produced by John Fogerty
Total running time: 29.25
Released in the US by Fantasy Records and
in the UK by Liberty Records

A phenomenon of the late '60s, Creedence Clearwater Revival's virtual demise in 1972 was universally regarded as being sadly premature.

The quartet formed in 1959, while they were all at El Cerrito high school in Berkeley, California, but they did not achieve significant commercial success until their 1968 revival of the Dale Hawkins rock classic, 'Suzie Q', went gold. They then accumulated 17 US hit singles, five of which also went gold, while four more went platinum.

With a classic beat-group line-up of two guitars, bass and drums, their hard-driving music was irresistible, especially because the youngest member, John Fogerty, was utterly brilliant at everything he undertook in the group: lead vocals,

lead guitar, songwriting, arranging and record production. This album was their third in just over a year, and their first to top the US chart, achieving platinum status like its predecessors. It included two big hits: 'Bad Moon Rising', their only UK Number 1, and the title track, both of which reached the US Top 3.

'Lodi' has become one of Fogerty's most-covered songs, with versions by Emmylou Harris, Tom Jones, Bobby Goldsboro and others. Another much-admired track on this album was the one non-original, the blues standard 'Night Time Is The Right Time'. Creedence's supercharged version with Fogerty's almost hysterical vocal (one of his trademarks) and a superb guitar solo with controlled feedback made this the version by which others are judged.

A RARE TALENT

John Fogerty's exceptional ability almost inevitably produced envy among his colleagues. His older brother, rhythm guitarist Tom Fogerty, bass player Stu Cook and drummer Doug 'Cosmo' Clifford, were content to allow him free rein until the end of 1970, at which point they could justifiably claim to be one of the biggest acts in the world.

Cosmo's Factory, their fifth album, had topped the US chart for nine weeks that year, but Tom Fogerty, who was four years older than the others, left the band in early 1971 to spend more time with his family, after participating on Pendulum, the group's sixth album in under three years. It dropped out of the US chart after a relatively brief residency, despite its eventual platinum status. This gave Clifford and Cook ammunition to demand greater involvement in subsequent albums. John Fogerty, now without fraternal support, felt obliged to concede.

The next album, 1972's Mardi Gras, was a typical result of compromise – it went gold, but failed to reach the US Top 10, and was described by a respected American critic as the worst album ever made by a major band. Later that year, the group fell apart, and it was all over. Only John Fogerty achieved anything of note subsequently, although he was inconsistent, artistically and commercially.

EASY RIDER

VARIOUS ARTISTS (1969)

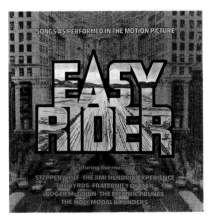

SONGS AS PERFORMED IN THE MOTION PICTURE

Producers not listed
Total running time: 37.42
Released in the US by Dunhill Records and
in the UK by Stateside Records

SIDE ONE
The Pusher (Axton) (1)
Born To Be Wild (Bonfire) (1)
The Weight (Robertson) (2)
Wasn't Born To Follow (Goffin/King) (3)
If You Want To Be A Bird (Antonia) (4)

SIDE TWO
Don't Bogart Me (Ingber/Wagner) (5)
If Six Was Nine (Hendrix) (6)
Kyrie Eleison Mardi Gras (Axelrod) (7)
It's Alright Ma (I'm Only Bleeding) (Dylan) (8)
Ballad Of Easy Rider (McGuinn) (8)

THE ARTISTS
(1) Steppenwolf, (2) Smith,
(3) The Byrds, (4) Holy Modal Rounders,
(5) Fraternity of Man,
(6) The Jimi Hendrix Experience,
(7) The Electric Prunes, (8) Roger McGuinn

Easy Rider was one of the quintessential feature movies of the '60s, not least because its soundtrack was packed with great music by the stars of the so-called 'underground' rock movement.

It starred Peter Fonda (who plays Captain America, a character whose motorcycle and jacket are decorated with stars and stripes) and Dennis Hopper as drug dealers who meet an alcoholic civil rights lawyer (an early starring role for Jack Nicholson).

The film climaxes when all three are murdered by rednecks. *Easy Rider* was an immense success due to its sympathetic view of hippie philosophies. It remains one of the genuine cinematic masterpieces to combine great music with a real plot and convincing acting.

Musical highlights included Steppenwolf's biker anthem, 'Born To Be Wild', Fraternity Of Man's 'Don't Bogart Me' (a song about the need to share a joint — marijuana cigarette — rather than monopolise it), and a wonderful version of 'Wasn't Born To Follow' by The Byrds (which featured superb phasing effects).

In the actual movie, The Band are heard performing their first hit, 'The Weight', but permission was not granted for their version to be on the soundtrack LP, and rather than omit the song entirely, a little-known group known as Smith recorded a cover version for the album.

MIXED FORTUNES

Of the acts who contributed to the soundtrack album, country rockers The Byrds and their leader, Roger McGuinn, have retained their mystique until today, despite the group breaking up in 1973.

The Holy Modal Rounders (Peter Stampfel and Steve Weber) continued to record occasionally through the '70s, but have never equalled the success they had with 'If You Want To Be A Bird'.

Steppenwolf, fronted by vocalist John Kay (real name Joachim Krauledat, who escaped from East Germany with his family as a teenager and settled in Toronto, Canada), formed in 1967 using the name Sparrow. They became Steppenwolf (after the Hermann Hesse novel) on signing with Dunhill Records. 'Born To Be Wild' (which includes the phrase 'heavy metal thunder', supposedly the source of the naming of the musical style) was included on their 1968 eponymous debut album. It was written by the exotically named Mars Bonfire (aka Dennis Edmonton, brother of the group's drummer, Jerry Edmonton).

'The Pusher', one of the first anti-drug anthems, was written by country star Hoyt Axton, whose mother, Mae Boren Axton, was one of the writers of Elvis Presley's first international hit, 'Heartbreak Hotel'.

THE BAND

THE BAND (1969)

Produced by John Simon
Total running time: 44.50
Released in the US & UK by Capitol Records

SIDE ONE
Across The Great Divide (J. R. Robertson)
Rag Mama Rag (J. R. Robertson)
The Night They Drove Old Dixie Down
(J. R. Robertson)
When You Awake
(R. Manuel/J. R. Robertson)
Up On Cripple Creek (J. R. Robertson)
Whispering Pines
(R. Manuel/J. R. Robertson)

SIDE TWO
Jemima Surrender
(L. Helm/J. R. Robertson)
Rockin' Chair (J. R. Robertson)
Look Out Cleveland (J. R. Robertson)
Jawbone (R. Manuel/J. R. Robertson)
The Unfaithful Servant (J. R. Robertson)
King Harvest (Has Surely Come)
(J. R. Robertson)

T he Band is packed with memorable songs inspired by tradition and history.

The choice tracks range from the American Civil War memoir of 'The Night They Drove Old Dixie Down' (covered by Joan Baez in 1971 and her only million-selling single) to the backwoods primitivism of 'Up On Cripple Creek' (the group's first US Top 30 single) and 'Rag Mama Rag' (their only UK Top 20 hit).

Even the black and white sleeve photograph with its sepia border seems antique, portraying the group as pioneering survivors of a bygone era in the history of America.

With most groups of the late '60s looking to the future rather than the past for inspiration, The Band's espousal of older values touched a nerve, not only among record buyers who made it the

group's only platinum album, but equally among their musical peers.

The name chosen by this quintet of mainly Canadian musicians was an indication of their low-key approach to both their music and stardom.

Their debut album, 1968's *Music From Big Pink*, was recorded in their house in Woodstock, where they were also backing Bob Dylan on demos of a rich vein of his new songs (released officially in 1975 by Dylan as *The Basement Tapes*, after they had been widely bootlegged).

For this follow-up, the group moved to California. The first LP had featured several songs by Dylan and three by keyboard player Richard Manuel. This one was dominated by guitarist Jaime 'Robbie' Robertson's compositions, although some were co-written with Manuel and drummer Levon Helm.

INSTRUMENTAL MAESTROS

The Band first assembled in the early '60s, when Robertson joined The Hawks, the group backing Canadian rocker Ronnie Hawkins. Drummer Levon Helm, a member of The Hawks since 1959, decided to stay in Canada rather than return to his native US, bass player Rick Danko joined in 1961 and keyboard players Richard Manuel and Garth Hudson were recruited later that year.

Albert Grossman, Bob Dylan's manager, hired them as Dylan's backing group on his 1965 world tour. This relationship continued sporadically until The Band broke up in late 1976 after a farewell concert at San Francisco's Winterland ballroom, recorded and filmed (by Martin Scorsese) as 'The Last Waltz' with Dylan, Hawkins, Eric Clapton, Neil Young, Van Morrison and many others guesting. One of The Band's features was their capability as multi-instrumentalists – on this eponymous album, group members played accordion, saxophone, trumpet, trombone, mandolin and violin as well as their main instruments.

BEST OF BEE GEES

THE BEE GEES (1969)

SIDE ONE
Holiday (Robin & Barry Gibb) *
I've Gotta Get A Message To You
(Barry, Robin & Maurice Gibb) **
I Can't See Nobody (Robin & Barry Gibb) *
Words (Barry, Robin & Maurice Gibb) **
I Started A Joke
(Barry, Robin & Maurice Gibb) **
Spicks And Specks (Barry Gibb) ***

SIDE TWO
First Of May
(Barry, Robin & Maurice Gibb) **
World (Barry, Robin & Maurice Gibb) **
Massachusetts
(Barry, Robin & Maurice Gibb) **
To Love Somebody (Robin & Barry Gibb) *
Every Christian Lion Hearted Man Will Show
You (Barry, Robin & Maurice Gibb) *
New York Mining Disaster 1941
(Robin & Barry Gibb) *

* A Robert Stigwood Production co-produced
by Ossie Byrne
** Produced by Robert Stigwood and
The Bee Gees
*** No producer credit
Total running time: 35.44
Released in the UK by Polydor Records and in the US by Atco Records

ontaining the cream of the early hits by the Gibb Brothers, the group's first gold album reached the Top 10 on both sides of the Atlantic.

Born on the Isle Of Man, Barry, Robin & Maurice Gibb first achieved fame in Australia, where they had emigrated with their parents in 1958. They returned to the UK at the invitation of London-based Australian impresario Robert Stigwood in 1967 and signed to Stigwood's production company.

Eight of the 12 tracks on the album were US Top 20 hits, while both 'Massachusetts' and 'I've Gotta Get A Message To You' were UK Number 1s.

The group's trademark fraternal harmonies and instantly commercial original songs, often in the style of The Beatles, quickly made them one of the biggest acts in the world.

Sibling rivalry forced Robin to quit for a solo career lasting eight months in 1969, before a reunion celebrated by the release of this collection. Initially a quintet completed by two Australians, guitarist Vince Melouney and drummer Colin Peterson, the reunited Bee Gees comprised only the three Gibb Brothers plus an anonymous backing band.

Although most of the tracks on this album were familiar to the great listening public, both 'I Can't See Nobody', and 'Every Christian Lion Hearted Man Will Show You' were relatively unknown.

A DUO ALONE

During Robin Gibb's absence from the group in 1969, Barry and Maurice Gibb not only released the unsuccessful 'Tomorrow Tomorrow' but also starred in 'Cucumber Castle', a feature film made by Robert Stigwood which included scenes shot in London's Hyde Park during the one and only British concert by the short-lived so-called supergroup, Blind Faith (formed by Eric Clapton and Ginger Baker, both from Cream, with Steve Winwood, ex-Traffic, and Ric Grech, previously of Family).

On 18 February 1969, Maurice Gibb married gravel-voiced Scottish vocalist Lulu, with his twin brother Robin as best man. The couple separated in 1973, and this was just one of the trio's problems during the first half of the '70s, which brought The Bee Gees only occasional minor hits. In 1975, they returned to the top of the US singles chart with 'Jive Talkin'', a hit which partially defined the disco era, as did their soundtrack to the 1977 feature film about New York nightclubs starring John Travolta, 'Saturday Night Fever' – the soundtrack album was certified eleven times platinum.

TROUT MASK REPLICA

CAPTAIN BEEFHEART & HIS MAGIC BAND (1969)

Produced by Frank Zappa
Total running time: 79.08
Released in the US & UK by Straight Records

An exceptional album, although it is impossible to verbalise the reason for its excellence.

Captain Beefheart (Don Van Vliet) is the ultimate '60s cult figure, whose disciples recognise him as original and unique. His extra-terrestrial vocal range of four and a half octaves is remarkable enough, but his astounding lyrics and his unlikely but effective mix of deep Delta blues and the avant-garde can leave listeners open-mouthed.

You have to hear for yourself 'The Blimp', for example, a taped telephone conversation in which Beefheart excitedly tells erstwhile schoolfriend, and this album's producer, Frank Zappa: 'It's the blimp, Frank, it's the blimp!', although we do not learn what it is.

The other musicians involved were all taught what to play by Beefheart, who also gave many of them new names: Zoot Horn Rollo (glass finger guitar and flute) is really Bill Harkleroad, and Antennae Jimmy Semens (steel-appendage guitar) is really Jeff Cotton.

The identity of The Mascara Snake (bass clarinet, vocal) is a mystery, but Rockette Morton (bass & narration) was Mark Boston and Drumbo (drums, of course) was John French, who had worked with Jeff Cotton in The Exiles, an R&B group from Lancaster, California (where Zappa and Beefheart went to school together).

For the 1968 *Safe As Milk* album, the Magic Band had enlisted the help of ace slide guitarist Ry Cooder, at the time a young Los Angeles prodigy.

Cooder recalled his time with the Captain in an '80s interview: 'Beefheart was having trouble with his guitar player at the time, who was suffering from nervous strain, which was brought about by Captain Beefheart!

'He had this record deal and they needed a little organisational assistance. He's an imposing figure and I started messing around with him, at his invitation, only to discover that it was like a hornet's nest, although he had great musical ideas.

'The Monterey Pop Festival was pending, and Bob Krasnow, who was an executive at Buddah, had the idea that it was going to be a big deal.

'We flew up to San Francisco, and on the way from the airport to Berkeley, Beefheart started to hyperventilate and get nervous – he's a hypochondriac, there's always something wrong with this guy: "Oh, I can't breathe, something's wrong, stop the car, I think I'm really sick. What did they put in my coffee on the airplane? I think they're trying to poison me."

'He went grey and white, and he turned all these colours, which was one thing he could really do, one of his things. We got up there... They introduced us, and we hit the stage and started into one of these insane numbers...

'During the second song, Beefheart starts to teeter towards the edge of the stage, holding his chest.

'He stops singing and comes walking back: "I'm going to fall down, I can't do

SIDE ONE
Frownland (Captain Beefheart)
The Dust Blows Forward 'n' The Dust
Blows Back (Captain Beefheart)
Dachau Blues (Captain Beefheart)
Ella Guru (Captain Beefheart)
Hair Pie: Bake 1 (Captain Beefheart)
Moonlight On Vermont
(Captain Beefheart)

SIDE TWO
Pachuco Cadaver (Captain Beefheart)
Bills Corpse (Captain Beefheart)
Sweet Sweet Bulbs (Captain Beefheart)
Neon Meate Dream Of A Octafish
(Captain Beefheart)
China Pig (Captain Beefheart)
My Human Gets Me Blues
(Captain Beefheart)
Dali's Car (Captain Beefheart)

SIDE THREE
Hair Pie: Bake 2 (Captain Beefheart)
Pena (Captain Beefheart)
Well (Captain Beefheart)
When Big Joan Sets Up (Captain Beefheart)
Fallin' Fitch (Captain Beefheart)
Sugar 'n Spikes (Captain Beefheart)
Ant Man Bee (Captain Beefheart)

SIDE FOUR
Orange Claw Hammer (Captain Beefheart)
Wild Life (Captain Beefheart)
She's Too Much For My Mirror
(Captain Beefheart)
Hobo Chang Ba (Captain Beefheart)
The Blimp (Captain Beefheart)
Steal Softly Thru Snow (Captain Beefheart)
Old Fart At Play (Captain Beefheart)
Veteran's Day Poppy (Captain Beefheart)

it, I've got to get out of here," and he falls off the stage into the grass on his face and just lies there!

'The people are cheering, because they can dig that, and the band's left onstage trying to play instrumentally but he wouldn't get up, claimed he had a heart seizure or whatever.

'There was no way a situation like that could be controlled, and finally I said "I quit, and I'm walking away from this, because it's too much for me."'

WEIRD YEARS

Little about Captain Beefheart is normal. His first single was released by A&M Records, but when he played the songs scheduled to appear on his first LP to one of the label's founders, he was told they were 'too negative'. Beefheart immediately freed himself from A&M by retiring for a year, until, in 1966, Bob Krasnow of Buddah Records agreed to put out the rejected album (which Beefheart re-recorded) as Safe As Milk. While recording the track 'Electricity' from that album, Beefheart's voice reputedly destroyed a $1200 microphone.

Trout Mask Replica's cover has Beefheart holding a trout's head in front of his face. While parts of it were being recorded at his house, he hired a tree surgeon to ensure that the nearby trees would not fall over because they were frightened by the music. Neither Zoot Horn Rollo nor Rockette Morton knew how to play musical instruments before they joined The Magic Band – Beefheart actually taught them to play. The 28 songs on the album were written at the piano (which Beefheart had never played before) in a continuous period of eight and a half hours.

IN THE COURT OF THE CRIMSON KING

KING CRIMSON (1969)

SIDE ONE
21st Century Schizoid Man including Mirrors
(Fripp/McDonald/Lake/Giles/Sinfield)
I Talk To The Wind (McDonald/Sinfield)
Epitaph including March For No Reason and Tomorrow And Tomorrow
(Fripp/McDonald/Lake/Giles/Sinfield)

SIDE TWO
Moonchild including The Dream and The Illusion
(Fripp/McDonald/Lake/Giles/Sinfield)
The Court Of The Crimson King including The Return Of The Fire Witch and The Dance Of The Puppets
(McDonald/Sinfield)

Produced by King Crimson
Total running time: 41.59
Released in the UK by Island Records and in the US by Atlantic Records

In 1968, a bizarre LP was released titled *The Cheerful Insanity of Giles, Giles And Fripp*, which supposedly sold well under one thousand copies.

After that the group, formed in Bournemouth, split up, and from its ashes came King Crimson, which included G,G&F members Robert Fripp (guitar), Mike Giles (drums), Ian McDonald (keyboards) and lyricist Pete Sinfield, with bass player/vocalist Greg Lake (ex-The Gods) replacing Pete Giles, who did not wish to join the new band.

After a long residency at London's Marquee Club in 1969, the group played on the bill of the legendary free concert in London's Hyde Park headlined by The Rolling Stones in July of that year, where their music was exposed to an audience estimated at 250,000.

This, their debut album, was released a few months later, reaching the UK Top 5 and the US Top 30, a considerable achievement for a debut, particularly as it so closely followed the disastrous Giles, Giles & Fripp debacle.

The two most outstanding tracks were the crunchingly heavy opener, '21st Century Schizoid Man', whose shorthand-styled lyrics seemed interestingly doom-laden, and the title track, a stately pomp-rock epic.

With an alarming sleeve – is it the 21st Century Schizoid Man (as the expression on the face suggests) or the Crimson King? – the album made an immediate impact, yet the group fell apart almost immediately.

Lake jumped ship to join keyboard player Keith Emerson and drummer Carl Palmer in forming the ELP supergroup.

A MUSICAL NURSERY

In 1976, Ian McDonald became one of the founder members of Foreigner, with whom he stayed for four years. Before they recruited Robert Fripp as guitarist, Pete & Mike Giles had led a band in Bournemouth with the extremely '60s name of Trendsetters Ltd. King Crimson can be seen in retrospect as a veritable nursery for latterday rock stars, as apart from Lake joining ELP and McDonald forming Foreigner, Boz Burrell, the vocalist and bass player in the group's fourth line-up (which began in late 1970) left to launch Bad Company with Paul Rodgers and Simon Kirke (ex-Free) and Mick Ralphs (ex-Mott The Hoople), and his replacement, John Wetton, left to join Roxy Music.

The drummer of the fifth line-up of King Crimson, Bill Bruford (ex-Yes), left to play with Genesis, Roy Harper, and Gong before forming a jazz/rock group, U.K., in 1977, which also included John Wetton. Fripp went on to make two albums with Brian Eno (ex-Roxy Music) and also worked with David Bowie on several albums in the late '70s/early '80s.

LED ZEPPELIN II

LED ZEPPELIN (1969)

Produced by Jimmy Page
Total running time: 40.24
Released in the US and UK on Atlantic Records

SIDE ONE
Whole Lotta Love (Jimmy Page/Robert Plant/John Paul Jones/John Bonham)
What Is And What Should Never Be (Jimmy Page/Robert Plant)
The Lemon Song (Jimmy Page/Robert Plant, John Paul Jones/John Bonham)
Thank You (Jimmy Page/Robert Plant)

SIDE TWO
Heartbreaker (Jimmy Page/Robert Plant/John Paul Jones/John Bonham)
Living Loving Maid (She's Just A Woman) (Jimmy Page/Robert Plant)
Ramble On (Jimmy Page/Robert Plant)
Moby Dick (John Bonham/John Paul Jones/ Jimmy Page)
Bring It On Home (Jimmy Page/Robert Plant)

The second Led Zeppelin album was as dynamic, exciting and loud as their debut LP, which had reached the Top 10 of the album charts on both sides of the Atlantic. Could a second album released only nine months later possibly be as good? Better – at least record buyers thought so. It topped the US chart for seven weeks and reached Number 1 in the UK.

Formed in 1968 as The New Yardbirds by guitarist Jimmy Page, Led Zeppelin included John Paul Jones, a session musician equally adept on keyboards and bass, and two musicians from the Birmingham area, vocalist Robert Plant and drummer John Bonham.

If Page was the best-known member of the group, his colleagues were equally skilled – the songwriting partnership of Page and Plant was an immediate success, while the rhythm section's composer credits on the familiar first track, 'Whole Lotta Love', suggest that their input was also significant.

Bonham's drum feature, 'Moby Dick', was not quite as sensational as his 30 minute (!) solo at New York's Carnegie Hall. 'The Lemon Song', with its line about squeezing the protagonist until the juice runs down his leg, was a perfect example of their roots and aims – simple lyrics over a solid Chicago blues. Hot guitar fills were set beside an impassioned vocal, with a middle passage when the tempo increases for a storming guitar solo before the vocalist's more measured return.

HOT AIR

Led Zeppelin (the name came from the comment made by one of the members of The Who that the group would go down like a lead balloon) encountered early problems in the use of the name. Countess Eva Von Zeppelin said that she found this noisy group using her family name annoying; as a result, the group played a Copenhagen concert using the name The Nobs.

'Whole Lotta Love' was arguably the group's best-known recording – a version of the song as recorded by CCS, a group fronted by British R&B pioneer Alexis Korner, was a UK Top 20 hit in 1970, and was used for some time as the theme tune to the extremely popular BBC-TV chart show, 'Top Of The Pops', although Page later said he rather disapproved of the CCS version.

Led Zeppelin never released a single in the UK. They felt it might detract from the impact of their albums, although pressure exerted by Atlantic Records resulted in ten US singles during the group's ten-year life. The biggest was 'Whole Lotta Love', which sold a million copies.

Robert Plant was not the first vocalist approached by Page, who initially contacted Terry Reid for the post. Reid wasn't interested and recommended Plant. He in turn suggested Bonham as drummer.

HOT RATS

FRANK ZAPPA (1969)

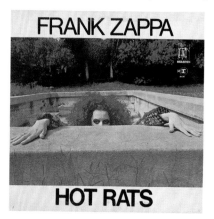

SIDE ONE
Peaches En Regalia (Zappa)
Willie The Pimp (Zappa)
Son Of Mr. Green Genes (Zappa)

SIDE TWO
Little Umbrellas (Zappa)
The Gumbo Variations (Zappa)
It Must Be A Camel (Zappa)

Produced by Frank Zappa
Total running time: 43.41
Released in the US on Bizarre Records and the UK on Reprise Records

Frank Zappa's experimental music was rarely accessible to record buyers. Early albums like 1968's largely orchestral *Lumpy Gravy* and the same year's *We're Only In It For The Money* were not mainstream LPs, but appealed to intellectuals and the elite.

The latter was a brilliant, although over-ambitious, lampooning of the hippie culture and its favourite album, *Sergeant Pepper* by The Beatles, with a carefully crafted parody of the latter's sleeve.

Lyrically obtuse and usually heavily cynical, and with instrumental flights of fancy from his band, The Mothers Of Invention, Zappa's work too often seemed admirable rather than enjoyable, and his always strange songtitles (eg 'Call Any Vegetable' and 'Brown Shoes Don't Make It' from 1967's *Absolutely Free* album) were viewed with suspicion by fans of the burgeoning psychedelic musical genre.

It came as quite a relief when *Hot Rats* emerged, because although the songtitles were still disturbing, the first two tracks were quite acceptable as state-of-the-art rock music.

It opened with 'Peaches', a cleverly arranged instrumental masterpiece which could easily be used as TV theme music. Zappa's buddy-in-arms Captain Beefheart was at his best vocally at the start of the bluesy 'Willie The Pimp'. That track also featured Don 'Sugarcane' Harris on violin and an extraordinarily long wah-wah guitar solo from Zappa himself. This was meaty music.

With violin virtuoso Jean-Luc Ponty on 'It Must Be A Camel', it was rather more user-friendly than other Zappa albums, which many found impenetrable (although few admitted it).

Even the disturbing sleeve prevented few from checking this out. It was Zappa's only UK Top 10 album, staying in the chart for over six months.

UNCONVENTIONAL INVENTION

Zappa was an anti-establishment figure from his teenage years – in 1955, at the age of 15, he developed a lifelong interest in the work of avant-garde composer Edgard Varese, whose music he had seen described as grotesque.

Balancing his love of R&B with his belief that provoking a reaction, positive or negative, was of paramount importance, Zappa refused to be predictable, musically or otherwise. He signed Alice Cooper to his sarcastically-named label, Straight Records, when they were rated the worst band in Los Angeles.

In 1969, at the London School Of Economics, Zappa was ready to answer questions after the screening of his film, 'Intercontinental Absurdities', but the session only drew out mutual distrust. The students wanted him to recommend a campaign of American-style civil disobedience as a continuation of their struggle with the college authorities. Zappa correctly noted that much more could be achieved by infiltrating the establishment (eg, becoming a lawyer or a doctor) than by destruction of property.

LET IT BLEED

THE ROLLING STONES (1969)

SIDE ONE
Gimme Shelter (Jagger/Richard)
Love In Vain (Woody Payne)
Country Honk (Jagger/Richard)
Live With Me (Jagger/Richard)
Let It Bleed (Jagger/Richard)

SIDE TWO
Midnight Rambler (Jagger/Richard)
You Got The Silver (Jagger/Richard)
Monkey Man (Jagger/Richard)
You Can't Always Get What You Want
(Jagger/Richard)

Produced by Jimmy Miller
Total running time: 43.12
Released in the UK by Decca Records and in the US by London Records

So much had happened for The Stones between 1968's *Beggars Banquet* and this follow-up album that it was remarkable that they managed to complete it at all.

When it did appear, it was apparent that it was in no way inferior to their previous successes. This was The Stones', and possibly rock's, peak in the '60s, despite it being released as the decade drew its final breaths. It entered the UK chart at Number 1 and achieved double platinum status in the US.

In June, Brian Jones had left the group, claiming that they had moved too far away from the blues for his liking. Next day came the announcement of his replacement, Mick Taylor, the 21-year-old lead guitarist from John Mayall's Bluesbreakers.

Both Jones and Taylor are credited as contributors, Jones with autoharp on 'You Got The Silver' and percussion on 'Midnight Rambler', Taylor with the much more audible slide guitar on 'Country Honk', the almost acoustic version of their single, 'Honky Tonk Women'. Nashville violin star Byron Berline also features on the album version.

Other American musicians on the album include Ry Cooder, who plays mandolin on the elderly blues cover, 'Love In Vain', Al Kooper, who shows off by playing piano, organ and French horn on 'You Can't Always Get What You Want', also featuring the ethereal vocal intro by The London Bach Choir (arranged by Jack Nitzsche) and with producer Jimmy Miller drumming in the absence of the great Charlie Watts.

BLOODY TIMES

The Stones played two historic free concerts in 1969, both of which were filmed, although the first was a triumph and the second a disaster.

In July, they played to 250,000 fans in London's Hyde Park, notable both for it being Mick Taylor's debut as a group member and for Mick Jagger's recital of Shelley's poem 'Adonis' in memory of Brian Jones, who had drowned two days earlier in the swimming pool of his mansion.

After this brilliant performance, Jagger and his girlfriend Marianne Faithfull flew to Australia. Both were to appear in movies, Jagger in the non-musical title role of 'Ned Kelly', the true story of a 19th Century Australian outlaw.

During the trip, Faithfull attempted to commit suicide (apparently because Jagger had told her that their romance was over). She remained in a coma for a week before recovering.

At the end of the year, the group tried to recreate their Hyde Park success with another free concert at Altamont Speedway in California. But their choice of the local Hells Angels chapter as security guards for the show proved to be a mistake. The Angels killed a young black audience member, Meredith Hunter, by stabbing him, a terrible climax to a sad and violent day which effectively marked the end of the peace and love era.

WOODSTOCK

VARIOUS ARTISTS (1970)

Produced by Eric Blackstead
Total running time: 132.21
Released in the US & UK by Atlantic Records

 lthough this triple album was not released until mid-1970, its presence here is explained by the fact that it represents the climax of the '60s.

It was recorded live at the August 1969 Woodstock hippie festival, when the culmination of the most important decade in 20th Century popular music took place on a farm in upstate New York owned by one Max Yasgur.

Although it was called the Woodstock Music & Arts Festival, it took place at Bethel, also in upper New York State. The site and facilities collapsed under the strain of an audience of up to half a million (with its requirement for food and sanitation) and heavy rain.

Nevertheless, Woodstock was a musical triumph. It made stars of John Sebastian, Richie Havens, Country Joe, Santana and Joe Cocker. It enhanced the reputations of Canned Heat, Crosby, Stills, Nash & Young, Sly & The Family Stone and Jimi Hendrix. And it gave Sha-Na-Na and Ten Years After a spell in the premier league.

It was also a disaster area for the huge audience, as 20 mile traffic jams built in the vicinity, and statistics tell us that in three days, 15-17 August 1969, there were three deaths, two births and four miscarriages.

Even so, Woodstock was the role model for all future rock festivals, both as the ultimate example of a new generation's hunger for influence, and its inability to organise and failure to pay attention to detail.

Many of the stars of the immediate future, the '70s, were there, including several acts who neither appear on this album, nor the 1972 follow-up double LP, *Woodstock II*: Blood, Sweat & Tears, The Grateful Dead, The Band, Creedence Clearwater (who apparently refused permission for their tracks to be included), Tim Hardin and some lesser names, who maybe weren't any good on the day.

There are many highlights on the album: Jimi Hendrix brilliantly desecrating the American national anthem, Joe Cocker's unforgettable version of 'With A Little Help From My Friends', and John Sebastian's archetypal tie-dyed hippie set.

On another level, it's interesting to note that the timing above relates to the music – there's nearly six minutes of crowd atmosphere as well, so this had

SIDE ONE
I Had A Dream (John B. Sebastian)
JOHN B. SEBASTIAN
Going Up The Country (Alan Wilson)
CANNED HEAT
Freedom (adapted from 'Motherless Child'
by Richie Havens) RICHIE HAVENS
Rock & Soul Music (Country Joe
McDonald/Barry Melton/Chicken
Hirsch/Bruce Barthol/David Cohen)
COUNTRY JOE & THE FISH
Coming Into Los Angeles (Arlo Guthrie)
ARLO GUTHRIE
At The Hop (A. Singer/J. Medora/
P. White) SHA-NA-NA

SIDE TWO
The 'Fish' Cheer/I-Feel-Like-I'm-Fixin'-To-
Die-Rag (Country Joe McDonald)
COUNTRY JOE McDONALD
Drug Store Truck Drivin' Man (Roger
McGuinn/Gram Parsons) JOAN BAEZ
featuring JEFFREY SHURTLEFF
Joe Hill (Earl Robinson/Alfred Hayes)
JOAN BAEZ
Suite: Judy Blue Eyes (Stephen Stills)
CROSBY, STILLS & NASH
Sea Of Madness (Neil Young) CROSBY,
STILLS, NASH & YOUNG

SIDE THREE
Wooden Ships (David Crosby/Graham
Nash) CROSBY, STILLS, NASH & YOUNG
We're Not Gonna Take It (Pete Townshend)
THE WHO
With A Little Help From My Friends (John
Lennon/Paul McCartney) JOE COCKER

SIDE FOUR
Soul Sacrifice (Carlos Santana/Gregg
Rolie/Jose Areas/Mike Carabello/David
Brown/Michael Shrieve) SANTANA
I'm Going Home (Alvin Lee)
TEN YEARS AFTER

SIDE FIVE
Volunteers (Paul Kantner/Marty Balin)
JEFFERSON AIRPLANE
Medley: Dance To The Music/Music Lover/I
Want To Take You Higher (Sylvester Stewart)
SLY & THE FAMILY STONE
Rainbows All Over Your Blues
(John B.Sebastian) JOHN B.SEBASTIAN

SIDE SIX
Love March (Gene Dinwiddie/Philip Wilson)
BUTTERFIELD BLUES BAND
Star Spangled Banner
(Trad. arr. Jimi Hendrix) JIMI HENDRIX
Purple Haze/Instrumental Solo
(Jimi Hendrix)

to be a triple album (a rare beast at any time). Released to coincide with the feature movie to which this was the soundtrack album, *Woodstock* topped the US chart for a month. It made a much less spectacular showing in the UK, not even reaching the Top 30, although its rather high retail price probably inhibited sales.

It is a measure of the precision (or luck) with which the Woodstock bill was assembled that 11 of the 16 acts featured on this album are also represented in this book in relation to their own albums. Of the remaining five, the most famous name is Santana, the jazz/rock group fronted by Mexican-born guitar virtuoso, Carlos Santana.

Their percussion-powered eight minutes plus 'Soul Sacrifice' was a highlight of the festival, and their eponymous debut LP, which was also released in 1969, achieved double platinum status during a US chart residency of over two years. Santana also supported The Stones at Altamont.

Carlos Santana later reminisced about Woodstock, the event which made him and his band an overnight sensation.

'We were very young, and it was a very wonderful time, before the concept of real hippies had been destroyed – a real hippy wasn't a harmful, dirty person, and it was a very constructive Bohemian type of thing between musicians and hipsters.

'I would define a hippy as somebody who would go from Joan Baez to The Grateful Dead to Miles Davis to Cream to The Beatles and back – people who were creative as artists and took pride in art, not in getting loaded and having free sex and all that dumb stuff.'

Sha Na Na were the surprise success – a giant (12 piece) rock'n'roll revivalist combo with four singers and an unforgettable and incredibly visual stage show. Their contribution to this album was a reasonably faithful copy of the 1958 doo-wop classic by Danny & The Juniors. The nature of their act meant that they made a greater impact live or on film than on this album.

The same was largely true of Ten Years After, a quartet from Nottingham whose spearhead was Alvin Lee, a lead guitarist who was one of the fastest (dozens of notes strung together at remarkable speed), but also one of the least inspired soloists of the era. The adrenalin generated by the event pumped up their live performance, but the group were average on record.

Richie Havens is also far better appreciated on stage than at home. 'Freedom' proves that while Woodstock was a feast for the eyes, it was, at times, famine for the ears.

Arlo Guthrie's father, Woody, is regarded as one of the most significant influences on '60s rock. He inspired both Bob Dylan and Donovan. Arlo rarely traded on his musical heritage, but attempted, with periodic success, to forge his own fame.

'Coming In To Los Angeles' was typical of his talents, a memorable song which has been interpreted as being about drugs, the subject of many songs in the late '60s.

While the '60s was undoubtedly the greatest decade in popular music, it left more debris in the shape of fatalities among its stars, the vast majority of which were not unrelated to drugs, than any other decade. A sobering thought.

THE END OF THE DREAM

Less than four months after Woodstock, with the hippie dream at its zenith, the bubble burst at another US festival, this time on the West Coast, at Altamont, where a similarly laissez-faire event starring The Rolling Stones became the scene for the death of an audience member, apparently beaten into oblivion by Hells Angels hired by The Stones as security guards.

Maybe fate refused to allow youth a second triumph over the establishment, or more likely indicated that life functions with much more certainty and safety when it is better organised, and that discipline often tends to be actually a help rather than a hindrance.

As a musical decade, the '60s displayed more innovation than any other of this century and possibly any since time began. The ultimate musical melting pot, it encompassed white and black musicians widely collaborating for the first time, broke down barriers (unfortunately subsequently re-erected, as today the record industry is controlled by a handful of giant multi-national corporations who rate profit as infinitely more important than music). It was also the midwife for stylistic cross-fertilisation (folk/rock, jazz/rock, country/rock, R&B/psychedelia and others) previously regarded as incompatible. It was a fabulous time to be alive.

Fortunately, with the introduction of the CD, the vast majority of the albums in this book are easily available in the '90s. There is therefore no necessity to pay exorbitant prices for antique vinyl.

During the '60s, the quality of the music improved too fast for the technology available. Three decades later, the tortoise has caught and passed the hare.